THE BARENTS REGION

EDITED BY
Ivar Bjørklund
Jakob J. Møller
and Per K. Reymert

UNIVERSITY OF TROMSØ
TROMSØ MUSEUM
1995

Front cover: Nenets camp, Bolshezemelskaja Tundra.
Photo: Ivar Bjørklund.

Back cover: Russian Pomor ships, Hammerfest, ca. 1900.
Photo: Wilse

Grafisk design: odahl grafisk design. Layout: Elisabeth J. Nilsen
Printed by: Lundblad Grafisk as, Tromsø

Contents

Foreword   3
Ivar Bjørklund

Novaya Zemlya – «No man's land»   4
Jens Petter Nielsen

Stalin's policy in the Arctic   18
Vladimir Nikolajevich Bulatov

The Pomor trade from a Norwegian perspective   26
Einar Niemi

The drum, the shaman and the world – shamanism in the north   37
Harald O. Lindbach

The Sami on the Kola Peninsula   48
Hans-Erik Rasmussen

The Russian Sami of today   56
Leif Rantala

Oil, gas and reindeer herding in the Nenets Autonomous Okrug   63
Johnny-Leo Ludviksen

A journey to the Bolshezemelskaja Tundra   71
Ivar Bjørklund

Foreword

WAY NORTH is a popular scientific publication from Tromsø Museum, the northernmost university museum in the world. Through WAY NORTH we want to introduce our English speaking visitors to the northern areas of Scandinavia and the Arctic. Our aim is to present the region's natural history, its inhabitants, their cultural heritage and their present way of life.

In this particular issue we will bring readers into the Barents Region: The northern parts of Norway, Sweden, Finland and Northwest–Russia. The articles focus on the cultural changes in this region. Being composed of many different ethnic groups, each with their own history and culture, the Barents Region presents a fascinating history of peaceful co–existence and a sustainable way of life. Whether we look at Norwegian fishermen, Sami or Nenets reindeer herders, Finnish farmers or Russian traders, they all managed their relations to the natural resources and to each other in such a way that living conditions for future generations were secured. Today, this is no longer the situation and in the following articles we want to take a closer look at the changes which have taken place. These include changes in Russian policy–making in the Arctic (Bulatov, Nielsen), as well as the decline in the old so–called Pomor trade between Russia and Norway (Niemi). Two of the articles cover the history and current situation of the Sami on Kola (Rasmussen, Rantala), while another gives an overview of shamanism as a religious belief in the northern areas (Lindback). Finally, the situation of the Nenets people faced with the development of the oil industry is presented (Ludviksen). You can also take part in a rather peculiar visit to a group of Nenets herders living way out on the tundra close to the Ural Mountains (Bjørklund).

Rob Barrett translated all the articles, some of which have been printed earlier in Norwegian in Tromsø Museum's publication OTTAR. The article by Hans-Erik Rasmussen is translated from the Danish publication JORDENS FOLK 1/1990, while the articles by Leif Rantala, Jonny-Leo Ludviksen and Ivar Bjørklund were written specially for WAY NORTH.

Tromsø, May 1995
Ivar Bjørklund

Novaya Zemlya – "No man's land"?

JENS PETTER NIELSEN

At the beginning of this century, the Arctic-faring skippers from Tromsø regarded the northern part of Novaya Zemlya as "no man's land" or *terra nullius*. **But wasn't it Russian territory?**

The Russians thought so, and their position was that their sovereignty of Novaya Zemlya, "the new land", was unquestionable. However there had long been some uncertainty, as no one seemed to know how far north Novaya Zemlya really stretched, and this weakened their position. Despite the fact that the Pomors had been hunting and trapping on Novaya Zemlya since the 16th century, and perhaps even earlier, the Russian authorities had no clear idea of the region's geographical shape. For example, in an atlas published by the Russian Academy of Science in 1737, Novaya Zemlya is drawn as a peninsula connected to the Taimyr.

However, in 1760 a trapper from Olonets, Savva Loshkin, sailed round the northern tip of Novaya Zemlya and thereby discovered that it was an island. In the 1820s and 1830s, Russian expeditions attempted to map the island in detail, but a series of accidents hindered the mapping of the northernmost part. After an expedition in 1838–39 failed completely, the authorities thought they would never penetrate further eastwards and thereby exploit the regions along the Siberian coast. In everyone's opinion the entrance to the Kara Sea was an impenetrable "ice-cellar". There was thus quite an uproar when, at the end of the 1860s, North Norwegian sealing vessels started to sail to Novaya Zemlya and, without any difficulty, continued into the Kara Sea. The first skipper to reach Novaya Zemlya was Elling Carlsen. He did so in 1867 with his vessel, the aptly named "Solid" of Hammerfest. Despite the Russian thinking at the time, he had no problems sailing some distance into the Kara Sea and returning through the Yugorsky Shar. From there he continued northwards along the coast until he reached Cape Nassau.

Norwegian trappers map Novaya Zemlya
The Norwegian push into Russian waters was a result of a rapid expansion of Norwegian arctic hunting. In the 1860s, the populations of walrus, seals and polar bears had started to decline on Svalbard, forcing the hunters to search further north and east into unknown waters. In 1869, 18 Norwegian vessels

with a total of 186 crew members hunted on Novaya Zemlya. One of the skippers was Edvard Holm Johannesen from Tromsø. On his return home, he sent a report of his travels with a summary of hydrographic readings to the Swedish Academy of Sciences in Stockholm. For his efforts, Johannesen was awarded the academy's silver medal.

The scientific interest of the Tromsø skippers resulted from contact with Swedish arctic explorers who, at the end of the 1850s and during the 1860s carried out large scientific expeditions to Spitsbergen and Greenland. The Swedes encouraged the Norwegian seamen to carry out accurate and systematic observations during their trips, and it was A.E. Nordenskiöld personally who awarded Edvard Johannesen his distinction for his observations in the East Ice in 1869. In the covering letter, Nordenskiöld also remarked that if Johannesen accomplished a circumnavigation of Novaya Zemlya, he would almost certainly be awarded the gold medal. When Nordenskiöld returned in the late autumn of 1870 from an expedition to Greenland, he did indeed receive a new report from Johannesen entitled "Hydrographic Observations during a hunting trip round Novaya

---

The first circumnavigations of Novaya Zemlya, made by sealers from Tromsø.

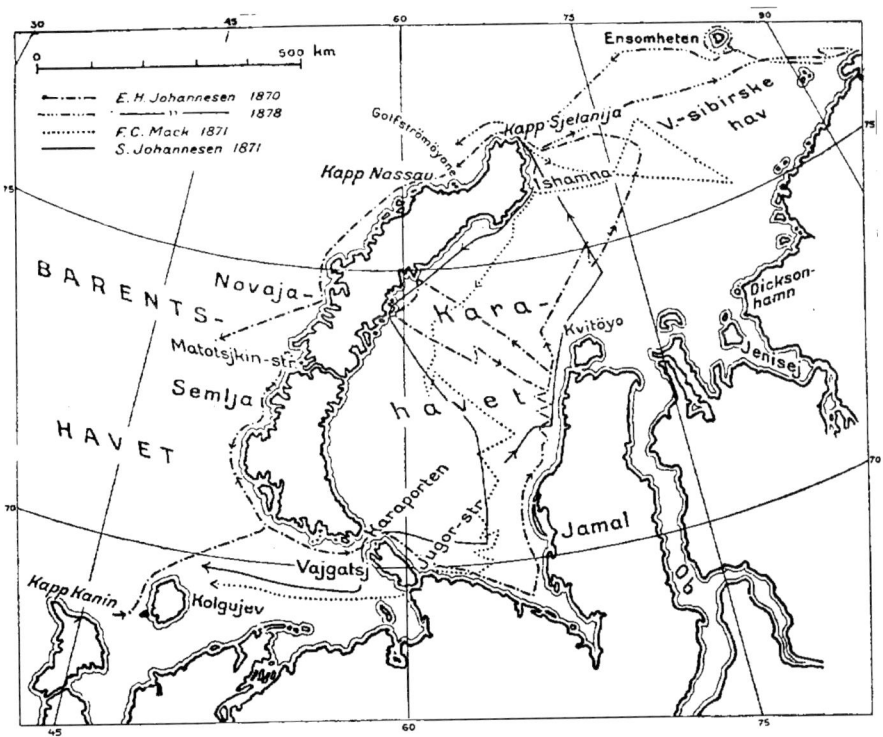

5

Zemlya". It turned out that Johannesen, during the summer of 1870, had had a very successful hunt. Instead of returning home immediately, he decided to attempt to win the prize Nordenskiöld had rather rashly promised him. First he headed northeast, but soon turned westwards towards the north coast of Novaya Zemlya, which he reached on the 3rd of September. From his boat, Johannesen then mapped the northern part of Novaya Zemlya and discovered that its coastline was very different to that previously described. He then returned to Norway after completing a voyage which, only a few years previously, had been considered impossible.

The Norwegians' hunting trips invalidated all earlier theories concerning the ice conditions east of Novaya Zemlya. Several vessels carried out remarkable voyages into the Kara Sea in the following years and, in 1871, Captain Fritz Christian Mack of Tromsø repeated Johannesen's feat and sailed north of Novaya Zemlya with his schooner "Polar Star". As data were gathered, the Norwegians' sketchmaps became incorporated in the charts of the seas around Novaya Zemlya, and on the basis of their collective observations, the Norwegian geographer and meteorologist Henrik Mohn published a map of the northern part of Novaya Zemlya. This map, in a way, summarized the Norwegian skippers' contributions to the mapping of the region.

The Northern Sea Route

The Norwegian expeditions to the Kara Sea served as the foundation for Nordenskiöld's opening up of the route to the mouths of the rivers Ob and Yenisei in 1875–76, and the complete navigation of the northern sea route in 1878–79. The Swedish-Norwegian consul general in Archangel referred to this in his correspondance with the Russian authorities concerning the frequent complaints about Norwegian activity in the Kara Sea. He maintained that the opening of the northern sea route would have enormous importance for future trade between Siberia and Europe, and as such it was meaningless to claim that the Norwegian activity did any harm to Russia.

But from the Russian point of view, the fact that North Norwegians carried out scientific observations during their voyages and, as such, had completed what the Russian cartographers had given

Captain Edvard Holm Johannesen, Tromsø.

up in 1840 was not to be considered to be a mitigating circumstance. Russian criticism was sharpened by the fact that the Norwegians were working under the guidance of Swedish scientists and that the opening of the northern sea route was portrayed as a result of a collective Scandinavian effort. Russia, the largest empire in the world, was left standing more or less as a passive spectator as foreigners solved the problem of opening the searoute from Europe to Siberia.

How heroic the Norwegian voyages into the Kara Sea actually were is a mute point, and one should be careful in describing these feats as a result of Norwegian valour or masterly seamanship. It is, all the same, true that the Russians, through their discoveries, had concluded (incorrectly) that the Kara Sea was not navigable and that this was proved wrong by the Norwegians. But one should point out that the Norwegians had been helped by very favourable ice conditions around 1870. The Soviet polar historian V.Ju. Vize is, of course, correct when he proclaims that it was equally wrong to claim that the Kara Sea was navigable as it was to claim it wasn't. The fact that the ice conditions were extremely difficult in 1872, causing the loss of seven of Tromsø's finest vessels and severe difficulties for others, is barely mentioned in the Swedish and Norwegian accounts.

Confrontation between Norwegians and Pomors

In 1874 ice conditions improved, and

From Novaya Zemlya. Painting by Ilya Vilka.

7

hunting increased. It is no exaggeration to say that the Norwegians dominated the East Ice in the following years. According to the Swedish-Norwegian consul general in Archangel, in 1870, 80-90 Norwegian vessels (most from Hammerfest) and only eight Russian ones took part in hunting around Novaya Zemlya and in the Kara Sea. The Pomors' excuse for their lack of participation was that they were held back by the Norwegians. They were not happy with the competition they faced, especially in an area which they considered to be indisputably Russian territory. Already in 1869, the brothers M.I. and F.I. Voronin of Suma had written to the Russian foreign minister complaining about the Norwegians' behaviour. They requested that hunting in the White and Kara Seas should be forbidden for Norwegians.

During the following years, there were several confrontations between Norwegians and Russians around Novaya Zemlya. The Norwegians were criticized heavily in the Russian press, and it was claimed that they were even threatening the Russians with violence. The Norwegian hunting expedition was depicted as a form of "polar sea imperialism". Norwegians considered Novaya Zemlya as "neutral territory" or "no man's land", as they did with Svalbard, and they systematically destroyed all Russian monuments, crosses and cabins in an attempt to undermine the Russians' right to the land. The time was now ripe for the Russians to retaliate and protect themselves against this Norwegian aggression.

Russian reserve
However, the Russian authorities did not intervene because they had no system for inspecting the hunting or fishing activities in the region. The huge distances and the lack of ice-free ports made it prohibitively expensive to keep military vessels in the area. Russia quite simply lacked enough funds to enforce an exclusion of foreign hunting on Novaya Zemlya, and the government did not want to declare any territorial borders as long as they could not protect them. The Russian foreign office also predicted that the Swedish-Norwegian authorities would retaliate, and this would have negative consequences for the Pomor trade and the Russian fishermen's rights in Finnmark. The official Russian reaction was so weak that the Finnmark district governor could not say with certainty whether Novaya Zemlya really was Russian territory or not.

The Norwegians were not, however, prepared to exploit this situation. In a letter to the Department of Internal Affairs in Kristiania dated the 3rd of March 1870, the Finnmark governor took up the Norwegian activity in the waters around Novaya Zemlya. He maintained that Norwegian activity in Russian territorial waters should be discouraged. But the problem was that nobody actually knew where the limits of these waters were, and repeated inquiries to the Russians yielded no answer. However, the Norwegian authorities were so keen to avoid any conflict with their mighty neighbour that they went so far as to draw up what they considered to be an equitable border (four nautical miles), and requested Norwegian skippers to respect it. So, although the local Pomor hunters failed to persuade the Russians to define their position concerning Novaya Zemlya with their complaints and actions, they did push the Norwegian authorities one step closer to accepting that the islands were indeed Russian.

One reason for the discontent was that Norwegian hunters had a clear advantage over the Pomors in that they could start their season at Novaya Zemlya earlier in the year. The Norwegian vessels could follow the ice-free route along the Murman coast and reach the hunting grounds at the end of April or beginning of May. The Pomors, on the other hand, had to wait for the ice in the White Sea to break up and could not reach Novaya Zemlya until about a month later, by which time the Norwegians had occupied the best hunting grounds. By the time the Pomors were able to start their hunt, the walrus and seals had become so nervous that they were difficult to approach.

Colonization of Novaya Zemlya

To make matters worse, other nations appeared on the scene towards the end of the 1870s. In March 1877, the Russian newspaper "Russky Mir" reported that a commission had been formed in the Hague by Prince Henric to collect money to erect monuments on all the Arctic

In the 1870´s the Tsar sent a group of Nenets to colonize Novaya Zemlya. In 1956 the island was made a nuclear testing site and the Nenets were forced to evacuate. (Photo: Ivar Bjørklund).

territories which they claimed had been discovered by Dutchmen. These territories included Novaya Zemlya. Soon afterwards there came reports of an expedition led by German scientists that was on its way to Novaya Zemlya to map the mineral deposits. They planned, along with Finnish partners, to form a company to exploit the resources of the region. Furthermore, the Austrians were also interested in the region and were apparently planning to establish a weather station on Novaya Zemlya.

Under these circumstances, an important initiative was taken by the Russian "Society for the Rescue of the Shipwrecked". The society sent a proposal to the Russian Ministry of Finance that a permanent rescue station be established at Malye Karmakuly on the southwest coast of Novaya Zemlya. Such an action would hopefully encourage the Pomors to follow their example and build winter stations at other sites on the islands. Their letter, signed by the society's patron, the grand duchess Maria Fedorovna, stressed the claims about Norwegian offences on Novaya Zemlya. This campaign by the society obviously made an impression and, in 1877, the Tsar granted 25,000 roubles towards building the rescue station.

The station was opened that same autumn, and was handed over to the Governor of Archangel a couple of years later. He then went a step further and encouraged colonization of the islands. However, it proved difficult to persuade Russian citizens to settle on Novaya Zemlya, and the governor diverted his attention to the Nenets (Samoyeds). Some Nenets were already living near Malye Karmakuly when the station was built, having been sent to Novaya Zemlya in 1867 from the Pechora district by a Russian trader. He had equipped them with modern weapons, but because the equipment had been lost or destroyed, the Nenets had not dared to return to the mainland. In 1883, some moved to the Matochkin Shar, the strait which divides Novaya Zemlya in two. From here it was easier to trap polar bears. To ensure a regular supply of provisions to these first permanent Russian subjects on Novaya Zemlya, a regular steamboat service was established in 1880 between Archangel and Novaya Zemlya.

The Nenets were thus "nominated" to be the foundation on which the permanent colonization of Novaya Zemlya should grow. With a colony of Nenets on the islands, the Russian authorities would have a better grip on the territory, and being a people of the Arctic, the Nenets had better abilities for adapting to the severe conditions than the Russians. In addition, the Nenets did not live in an area spread over several countries, as was the case with the Sami people and whose national affiliation was rather this ambiguous. The Nenets were a purely "Russian" minority, and their colonization of Novaya Zemlya could be considered in effect a Russian occupation.

By 1898, 22 Nenets families (102 persons) lived on Novaya Zemlya – 12 in Malye Karmakuly, six in the Matochkin Shar and four in Beluzhya Guba. The governor took upon himself to provision them with all their needs. In return, the Nenets were obliged not to trade with anyone except a representative of the government. Their products were sold at market price in Archangel, and the income was used to cover the costs of their provisions. Any profits, apart from a little fund put aside for further colonization, were payed to the Nenets.

Abroad, this set-up was interpreted as a form of monopoly, along the same lines as the Danish rule on Greenland. The authorities attempted a kind of «Russianization» of the Nenets, and the Orthodox Church was to play a major role in the conversion of the Nenets into "useful Russian citizens". Father Iona of the Nicholas Korel monastery was sent to Novaya Zemlya in 1877 by the Bishop of Archangel. His task was to preach to the Nenets, educate them, and prepare them for the transformation from a nomadic lifestyle to one of permanent settlers. In 1899, the Holy Synod even decided to establish a modest hermitage on the islands.

A cruiser is deployed

The Russians thus gave priority to a consolidation on Novaya Zemlya rather than to antagonism; surveillance and control of Norwegians was not considered important enough to justify the costs and tensions in Russia's relations with Norway. But in 1891, the situation changed when Tsar Alexander III decided to build a railway across Siberia to the Far East. The government was determined to complete the building of the Trans-Siberian railway in the shortest time possible. The building

---

*Nenets on Novaya Zemlya.
Painting by Ilya Vilka.*

materials were transported overland to the Urals and by sea to the ports of the Far East, but the problems of transporting rails and other materials through the roadless terrain were almost impossible to solve. The Naval Ministry thus proposed that an attempt be made to open a sea route from Archangel and over the Kara Sea to the mouth of the Yenisei and onwards up the river. This resulted in increased attention being drawn to the northern regions.

A cruiser was deployed to carry out hydrographic surveys east of the White Sea and to gather data neccessary to determine the possibilities for such a sea route. It was also decided that the same cruiser should keep an eye on the Norwegians who were hunting in the region. After raising the question with the Swedish-Norwegian authorities, the Russian foreign minister was convinced that the Norwegian authorities would not support their countrymen if a conflict concerning the territorial borders arose – nor did they when seven Norwegian vessels were impounded in 1893 for illegal hunting in the White Sea.

But further east, at Novaya Zemlya, the Norwegians were not so bothered about the presence of the Russian cruiser, and in the early 1900s Norwegian activity on the East Ice increased considerably. Nearly half the Norwegian fleet of sealers worked there, and their activity started to undermine the system of reserves on the islands. Furthermore, some doubt had arisen considering the Nenets' patriotism. In 1902–03, a Norwegian scientific expedition wintered on Novaya Zemlya near the western end of the Matochkin Shar. The expedition, led by the geophysicst H. Riddervold, was one of four carrying out Professor Kristian Birkeland's northern lights research programme.

An appeal to Oscar II

Not unexpectedly, the Norwegians soon came into contact with the Nenets who soon took advantage of this contact with a foreign power and complained about their treatment by the Russian authorities. A spokesman who claimed his opinion was representative of the feelings of all the Nenets on Novaya Zemlya stated that the conditions under which they lived had become so difficult that their only means of salvation was through Norway annexing the islands. He asked the name of the Norwegian king, and when told that it was Oscar II, came out with the following appeal:

"Please greet Oscar and ask him to send men here to take Novaya Zemlya from the tsar because we Nenets are in great difficulty; we lack everything, have no flour, sugar or tea, while the Russian officials are lining their own pockets!"

The Swedish-Norwegian consul general in Archangel, H.A. Falsen, reported that the problem on Novaya Zemlya was that the Nenets were not inclined to increase their hunting because they were at one time singled out as the government's "pets". Nor were they certain that they were being treated fairly by the governor's administrative officer who controlled the sale of their products.

But the Russian authorities had another view. The problem was not the Nenets' laziness, but the fact that they traded most of their products with the Norwegians. And the governor of Archangel had a strong impression that much of the bartering was "encouraged" by bottles of rum. When the administrative officer visited Novaya Zemlya in the summer of 1908 in Pomor Bay near Matochkin Shar, he came across two Norwegian vessels, the "Silver" and the "Success". On board he found no fewer than 29 polar bear cubs, around 1000 seal skins and 2,500 pounds of blubber. Most of the goods were acquired through trading with the Nenets. The Russians felt very provoked by this and complained to the Norwegian authorities through Consul General Falsen.

But this made little impression on the Norwegian hunters, who were taking advantage of the confusion surrounding the actual position of the Russian border. They had noticed that the Russian inspection vessel never ventured north of the Matochkin Shar, and when skipper Sivert Brœkmo met the warship "Pakhtusov" in the Vaigach Strait in the summer of 1902, he took the opportunity to ask where the border really was. The ship's captain traced it on the map and claimed that it stretched three nautical miles off the coast north to Sukhoi Point, which is eight nautical miles north of the Matochkin Shar. North of this point, the Norwegians could hunt both on land and at sea. The line was drawn on the skipper's chart, and the commander even put his signature to it. Brœkmo naturally took this as an official Russian

Grigori Nikolajevitsj Valej – a singer of Nenets legends. (Photo: Ivar Bjørklund).

13

confirmation that the northern part of Novaya Zemlya was "no man's land", as Svalbard was at the time. In the years immediately after 1905, several Norwegain expeditions went so far as to winter on Novaya Zemlya, even using some of the old Russian trapping stations.

An unexpected meeting
The Russian authorities were obviously ignorant of this activity, and did not intervene until the Russian Agricultural Ministry sent an expedition to the islands in 1909, under the leadership of the geologist V.A. Rusanov. Rusanov had visited Novaya Zemlya in 1907, but only the southern part of the island. This time he was sent to study the geology, biology and meteorology along the coast between Krestovaya Bay and Admiralty Peninsula. When his research vessel, the "Dmitry Solunsky" steamed into Krestovaya Bay, the crew noticed a couple of trapper's huts with people wandering between them and smoke rising from the chimneys. Rusanov and some of the crew assumed they were Russians and rowed ashore. They were somewhat surprised not only to find that the hunters were Norwegians, but also that, because of a successful hunting season, these intruders had planned to spend another winter there. The Norwegians were very hospitable however, and the parties separated with ostensibly the best relations.

But inwardly Rusanov was shocked and in his log wrote, "A sad sight on Russian territory! There, where our brave Russian Pomors have hunted for centuries, Norwegians now live undisturbed and gather riches". On his return to Archangel, he reported all that he had seen to the governor, who immediately sounded the full alarm. The Russians regarded the Norwegian residency as a true threat to Russian sovereignity of the region, since it could be interpreted as an occupation. As far as the Russians were concerned, Novaya Zemlya had been Russian territory since time immemorial, and on the 15th of November 1909, the Russian amabassador in Kristiania delivered a note of protest to the Norwegian Foreign Ministry. The Norwegians were requested to investigate the case and inform the people of North Norway that similar violations of Russian territories would not be tolerated.

Tromsø skippers mobilize
This was the sharpest protest the Norwegians had ever received from Russia, and in Kristiania the situation was taken very seriously. This was especially so because reports from the skippers revealed that Norwegian activity on Novaya Zemlya was far more extensive than the Russians were aware of. But it proved to be a very difficult case to solve. The Norwegian skippers reacted angrily and called a meeting of the so-called "Association of Tromsø Skippers" on the 8th of February 1910 to discuss the situation. Most of those who had hunted on Novaya Zemlya voiced their opinion and all claimed that Norwegians had hunted there undisturbed for nearly half a century. They also referred to Brœkmo's map which had been drawn up by the commander of the "Pakhtusov" and which showed that the border ran just north the Matochkin Shar, making the land to the north free.

The association passed a powerful resolution in which they ascertained that, if the Russians wished to take possession of this part of the Arctic, the case should first be decided by an international court. In the minds of the skippers, there was no doubt that the northern part of Novaya Zemlya was "no man's land", as was Franz Josef Land, Spitsbergen and the northern part of Greenland. The association's unanimous opinion was that Novaya Zemlya, north of Matochkin Shar, was international territory, since Norwegians had hunted there for decades without any interference from the Russians.

This resolution was published in the newspaper "Tromsø Stiftidende" and the news soon reached Russia. The "Tromsø Resolution" was sharply condemned in the Russian press and, on the 20th of March 1910, the Norwegian Foreign Ministry received yet another note from the Russians, a note with an unusually sharp and ironic wording. The Russian government stressed that in no way was the claim that Novaya Zemlya was "no man's land" correct. They stated that the Norwegian and other governments were in full agreement that the whole of Novaya Zemlya was an integral part of the Russian Empire.

The Norwegian Foreign Minister was informed that if any hunter continued to claim otherwise, it would lead to the confiscation of his catch and equipment at the very least. The Norwegian hunters' inexplicable ignorance could cause them a lot of trouble. Such a warning was timely, as the Russians soon got wind of

Nenets on Novaya Zemlya. (Painting by Alexander Borisov).

more Norwegian winter expeditions which had reached Novaya Zemlya. It was decided at high governmental level in Russia, to send a warship to evict these expeditions, either peacefully or by force. The Tromsø Resolution had turned the situation into a matter of principle which could not be solved in any other way.

An appeal to Nicholas II
There was little the Tromsø skippers could do when faced with this demonstration of power, except salvage what they could. They became worried about the fate of those who were still on Novaya Zemlya and decided that a rescue party should be mounted. After negotiations with the Foreign Ministry and at governmental cost, the steamer "Sirius" was sent from Tromsø on the 14th of June to inform the Norwegians on Novaya Zemlya of the situation and the danger they faced. Meanwhile, King Håkon, on the advice of the Consul General in Archangel, composed a letter to his relative, Nicholas II, in an attempt to calm the situation down. There is reason to believe that this letter actually helped; the Tsar soon intervened by stopping the warship and sending a civilian research vessel instead. On board was the Governor of Archangel and four Russian families from the Shenkursk region who had agreed to settle in Krestovaya Bay as colonists. The expedition discovered five Norwegian huts, one in Nordenskiöld Bay, three in Archangel Bay and one in Krestovaya Bay, which the ship entered on the 15th of July. However, there was no confrontation, since the Norwegians had already abandoned the area, obviously in great haste. The Governor wished to show the significance of the Russian case and in a ceremony laid the foundation stone of the first house in Krestovaya Bay. Once done, the establishment of the "first Russian colony" on the northern part of Novaya Zemlya was celebrated with champagne.

A final settlement
The diplomatic crisis of 1909–1910 was perhaps the most serious episode ever to arise in the relations between Norway and the Russian Tsardom which, for centuries, had been characterized by peace and tolerance. It was solved by restraint from both sides. The decisive factor was that the Norwegian government did not in any way support its own subjects' pretensions concerning Novaya Zemlya. It was prepared to "render unto Caesar the things that are Caesar's" and, in November 1910, the county governors in Finnmark and Troms composed a warning to be hung up on all vessels. This notice clearly stated the official Norwegian view concerning the sovereignty of the islands: "[The Norwegian Government] hereby declares that the whole of Novaya Zemlya is Russian territory, and that Norwegians who hunt there or in the territorial waters around the islands, may be subjected to the confiscation of their catch and vessel, as well as to unpleasant consequences for themselves personally".

The Russians received a copy of this notice and had good grounds to be satisfied. Another episode was over. Ironically, the people of Northern Russia had also good cause to thank the

Norwegian hunters who, through their audacious behaviour, had provoked the Russian government to act. It had to decide whether or not it wanted to keep what had for a long time been considered a Russian possession. Thus Norwegian fishing and hunting in Russian waters helped increase Russian commitment in the northern territories towards the end of Russia's old regime.

Jens Petter Nielsen,
Institute of Social Science,
University of Tromsø,
9037 Tromsø.

Stalin's policy in the Arctic

VLADIMIR NIKOLAJEVICH BULATOV

Josef Vissarionovich Stalin had a special interest in the Arctic, especially the northern sea route and the huge areas bordering it. We shall see here what consequences this had for the region, the people and the environment.

After "the great year of change", 1928, and the historic changes that were associated with the implementation of the five-year plan, Stalin was convinced that no challenge was too great for him. It was then that he uttered the famous greeting to the members of the 1932 expedition on icebreaker "Sibiryakov": "Your expedition, which has overcome the almost impossible obstacles, has, with its success, shown that there are no barriers strong enough to resist the Bolshevik bravery and organisation". But what Stalin failed to notice was the fact that the people involved faced huge losses when breaking down these barriers. Furthermore, not all obstacles necessitated such an attack.

Glavsevmorut (GUSMP)
In December 1932, a special conference was held in the Kremlin. Among the participants were the members of the "Sibiryakov" expedition, the Party and the government, and officials from several People's Commisariats. Stalin gave a speech which outlined the Soviet state's policy regarding the exploitation of the northern sea route and the lands bordering it. A few days later, on the 17th of December, the Soviet government passed a resolution to organize a special directorate for issues concerning the northern sea route. This directorate was under direct governmental control. The objective of the GUSMP (The Chief Directorate for the Northern Sea Route) was to "definitively open the northern sea route from the White Sea to the Bering Strait for traffic, to equip it with the necessary installations, and maintain them to ensure a safe journey along the route".

After the crew of another icebreaker, the "Chelyuskin", returned, another conference was held. Again, Party and government leaders took part, as well as representatives of the Peoples' Commisariates. At one of these conferences, Stalin gave a speech about the GUSMP and the role he thought it should play. He recommended that an institution based on the model of the old Dutch East India Company be founded in the northern regions; with such a set-up, he could give the GUSMP full control over the north's economy, as well as the relevant scientific and cultural affairs. In 1934, a resolution "Concerning enterprises for the development of the Northern Sea Route and for the Economy of the Northern Regions" was passed by the Party's Central Committee. The Directorate for the arctic regions took control of the economy and culture of the more distant regions in the north. Many ventures were initiated. The supply and trade of goods was started, and special concessions were given to start businesses on the islands in the arctic seas. Investments were also made in the search for and exploitation of the natural resources in the Arctic.

Shipwrecks and their consequences
However, Stalin and the Party's Central Committee constantly intervened in the business of the GUSMP. They made decisions concerning the northern regions over the heads of those originally delegated to do so. This interference not only led to confusion, but it was also illegal. It greatly upset the balance in the influence between the Party's and country's economic organisation apparatus for the northern sea route and the northern regions.

The events which soon followed demonstrated the damage this excessive centralization had on the activities of the GUSMP. 1937 was a catastrophic year. Nearly the whole of the GUSMP fleet had to be abandoned while overwintering in the Arctic, for a variety of reasons.

The ice conditions along the northern sea route were especially difficult, and incompetence and stupidity reigned in the team in charge of the maritime operations. As if this wasn't enough, S.A. Levanovsky disappeared with his plane as he started a propaganda tour over the Atlantic to the USA . As a result, several icebreakers and nearly the whole airforce in the polar regions were sent out to search for his plane.

Stalin was not slow in reacting, and did so on two fronts. One was to find "enemies of the people, spies and saboteurs". The other was a partial

Josef Vissarionovich Stalin. (NTB).

reorganization of the GUSMP. On the 29th of August 1938, the Council of People's Commissaries discussed the question of "how to improve the work of the GUSMP". The debate ended in a government resolution in which the attention of polar scientists was drawn to the importance of solving the main problem of making the northern sea route a safe and functional option.

People's heroes

The conquering of the Arctic and the opening of the northern sea route played a significant role in the minds of the Soviet people. With jubilation, they monitored the progress of Papanin and his crew as they drifted out to sea on an icefield. They followed wholeheartedly the soon-to-be legendary expeditions of the icebreakers "Sibiryakov", "Chelyuskin" and "Litke", and were on Christian-name terms with the arctic pilots – who became the first heroes of the Soviet Union.

Many generations of Soviet children were brought up on the stories and legends of the heroic activities of Soviet polar explorers. However, in parallel with this heroism, a long string of events unknown to the masses occured – irresponsible decisions, risk-taking, and heavy oppression. On the one hand, these other events were ingeneously concealed behind pompous meetings held in honour of the polar heroes, ceremonies and presentations of decorations. On the other hand, they involved hundreds of scientists, seamen and pilots. This was

---

Stalin meets members of a polar expedition on the Red Square, Moscow 1934.

Stalin's policy in the Arctic – a policy which has been little studied.

The other side of the picture

The well-known pilot I.P. Mazuruk, who was also a hero of the Soviet Union, has pointed out one characteristic of Stalin: "Stalin always understood with masterly ingenuity how to take advantage of the fruits of our work in the Arctic. Any meaningful event was used to his advantage. We, who had earned our decorations and medals with our blood, were rewarded generously, and with the help of these medals he blinded those who tried to discover what was really going on in the country. In this way the enthusiasm and the valur of our people, and especially the arctic explorers, camouflaged the criminal actions that were being carried out at an ever increasing rate."

Among those arrested who met their fate were a series of known personalities connected to the Directorate for the Northern Sea Route: N.I. Pakhomov, People's Commissioner for Sea and River Transport; S.A. Bergavinov, head of the political Underdirectorate of the GUSMP; N.N. Kuzmin, leader of the Archangel Territorial Management of the GUSMP; R.L. Samoilovich, Director of the Arctic Institute; and B.V. Lavrov, who built the industrial plants at Igarka and Nordvikstroj. The blood-thirsty executioners showed no mercy, not even for the heroes of the "Chelyuskin". Of

The Wellmann-expedition to Franz Josefs Land, 1898. (Photo: Tromsø Museum).

these, A.N. Bobrov, I.Ja. Bayesk and P.M. Khymyznikov were arrested; they were later executed or died in jail.

The mining city of Kirovsk. (Photo: Øyvind Sundheim).

Industry and labour camps

The opening of the northern sea route had a decisive role in the economic development of the polar region. Industry was started on a huge scale, and towns, ports and workers' colonies were built far north of the Arctic Circle.

In the 1930s, the Soviet northern regions initiated a system of so-called labou- and improvements camps where the internees were "retrained through work". The prisoners toiled and struggled on the building sites from The White Sea canals to Vorkuta. They built towns and industrial plants in the far north, worked in the forests in the Archangel region and Karelia and in the mines and oil production plants in the Ukhta and Pechora region, and they built roads through the nearly impenetrable taiga and over the endless tundra.

One of the most remarkable feats carried out during the conquering of the Arctic was the establishment of heavy industry in the form of huge and complex industrial conglomerates. And with this grew a series of associated enterprises, such as power stations, a food industry, housing for the workers, etc.

The first of these territorial conglomerates, as they were called, was built at Khibinogorsk on the Kola Peninsula. Khibinogorsk, today called Kirovsk, was built during the five-year period prior to the Second World War. It was an enrichment plant for the minerals apatite and nepheline and, within a year, produced two million tonnes of apatite concentrate. The huge conglomerates "Severonikkel" and "Kolstroj" were also built during this period.

Norilsk

Thanks to the development of the northern sea route, the industry in Yakutia, Kolyma and Magadan also expanded dramatically. Another area where industries expanded was the region around the towns of Ukhta and Pecha. At the same time, the pride of Soviet industrialization, Norilsk, took off. This industrial town in the northeast first produced coke, and later metals.

Forced labourers, the victims of Stalin's policy of oppression played a significant part in the establishment and development of the huge industries in the northern parts of the Soviet Union. During the first two years of the Directorate of Arctic Areas, the quarries and metal founderies in Norilsk were established. Later the responsibility for them was handed over to a special organization called Norilskstroi. Tens of thousands of workers were brought in from the surrounding district to build up not only the metalurgic plant itself but also the town in which the workers were housed. Among the prisoners was N. Urvantsev, a skilled geologist who was one of the first to discover nickel in the mountains near Norilsk. Another prisoner was A. Milchakov, who was one of the secretaries general of the Party's Central Committee and the youth organization Kosmomol. Also included were famous authors and writers such as Aleksei Garri and Evgeny Ryabchikov, the poet David Kugultinov, the Soviet artist Georgy Zhzhenov, and many others.

Many of the workers in Norilsk died of exhaustion, malnutrition, scurvy or influensa-like illnesses. Many others were executed.

The labour camps in Norilsk, the Norillag, were an integral and vital part of the northern sea route project. To the east, the Norillag bordered onto the camps along the River Lena, which in turn reached east to the camps in Kolyma. Even before the Second World War, the labour camp system covered the whole of the Taimyr Peninsula: iron ore mines and enrichment plants in full production, railways which transported ore to Dudinka, coal mines which were established at junctions along the northern sea route to provide the ships with coal, and the salt mines at Nordvik which supplied Norilsk. As we now know, it was not only the Arctic zone heroes who founded Sevmorput – the northern sea route and the surrounding industries. Besides those we know from pictures in film clips and the daily press, in reality, there were also the tens of thousands, perhaps even hundreds of thousands of slaves who toiled daily to conquer the northern sea route – all anonymous and sentenced "for political reasons, but without investigation and trial".

A.P. Zavenyagin

We should mention here the role played by Avramy Pavlovich Zavenyagin, who was at the organizational forefront during the development of this Soviet industry. Soon after he became director and responsible for the development of this gigantic polar conglomerate, he established a planning department which was of unconceivable dimensions for that time. It had more than 600 members of staff, and its role with regard to the technical functions during further industrialization can not be overrated. For several especially well-qualified employees, the department acted as a haven. The paper "Pravda" later wrote of Zavenyagin: "He saved many.....This was not private benevolence. He gave the weak courage and the desperate hope, to us all he gave the belief that our work meant something. He gave the people the best he could give – a goal and a meaning of life".

Igarka

The building of Igarka started in 1929. This project was something completely new within town planning and building: never before had a town been built in a region of permafrost. And this town north of the Arctic Circle was soon to have several thousand inhabitants. In 1930 the first sawmill opened, by 1932 another two were operating, and together they produced 25,000-30,000 different "production standards".

But the establishment of Igarka also had its drawbacks, which were directly connected to the collectivization of the country. The journal "Sovyetskaja Arktika" remarked in 1936: " The inhabitants of Igarka were banished from their homelands; most of them took up honest work for the first time in their lives, work which was not based on the exploitation of others".

Graves on the tundra. (Painting by Alexander Borisov).

Another article, describing the history of industrialization in Igarka, described Zinovy Chuchalin as being "previously a landowner and farmer who was expelled to Igarka at the wishes of the collective farmers in his own village. In Igarka he went through two years of proletarian indoctrination. He worked as a labourer. This year he was appointed foreman". Igarka became not only one of the "grand socialist experiments" of the Arctic, but also a destination for the banished who were the first victims of Stalin's reprisals. This arctic town was not only built by the hard work and enthusiasm of the locals and voluntary immigrants from the south, but also with the sweat and blood of the thousands of innocent people convicted during the years of Stalin's personality cult.

Ecological consequences

When we describe the industrialization of the north, we can not ignore the consequences it had. No thought was given to the environment, which we now know is especially sensitive in polar areas. As a result, we now have dead forests around Norilsk, lifeless lakes on the Kola Peninsula (especially around Apatity), thousands of tonnes of industrial waste, technical equipment, etc. on the islands and shores of the polar seas, and greatly mismanaged fish and other marine resources in this region.

But even today, we continue to destroy the thin layer of soil on the open tundra and in the forests as we drive around in tracked vehicles or carry out other damaging industrial incursions. We continue to destroy the sensitive equilibrium of the arctic environment in exactly the same way as we did during the years of industrialization.

Conclusions

When drawing conclusions about Stalin's policy in the north, we have to admit that during this period, which in historical perspective is extraordinarily short, Stalin not only succeeded in establishing a safe transport route through the northern parts of European Russia, Siberia and the Far East; he also established an effective means of harvesting the natural resources and developing new production plants in these arctic regions .

However, this cost an unbelievable number of Soviet lives, resulted in huge material expenses, and led to ecological catastrophes we are still struggling with. This was the direct result of Stalin's personal policy in the Arctic.

Vladimir Nikolajevich Bulatov,
Dept. of History
Pomor University,
Archangel,
Russia.

The Pomor trade from a Norwegian perspective

EINAR NIEMI

The Pomor trade has always been discussed in North Norway in positive terms; the trade was a blessing for the people and the region. There is even a strong tradition of seeing this trade not only as positive but even crucial in enabling people to prosper along long stretches of the North Norwegian coast: "I'll tell you straight. If it the Russians hadn't bought our fish, then we would have had to move elsewhere".

Today – with the recent opening of relations between east and west – we see a return of the term "Pomor" as a result of the survival of this tradition. The term is regarded positively on both sides of the border, and "Pomor" is associated with contact and cooperation between North Norway and Northwest Russia, with friendship, development and interdependence. The term is now turning up in a variety of contexts – on the Russian side in "Pomor choir", "Pomor University", on the Norwegian side in "Pomor days", "Pomor museum", names of companies, etc.

But how was the Pomor trade regarded during its heyday? Were people unanimously positive? What did it entail and were there varying interests?

An ancient trade
The Pomor trade dates far back in Nordkalotten. It was originally and for a long time referred to as the "Russian" trade; few knew it as the Pomor trade. It was only later that authors, journalists and scientists started calling it this, and then not really until the end of the 1800s. Trade between northern Russia and Norway dates back to the days of the sagas, when North Norwegians and representatives of the Norwegian crown travelled eastwards to the mouth of the Dvina, to the famous market at Kholmogory. This trade ceased in the 13th century. However, in the late Middle Ages new trading possibilities arose, especially at the markets along the Arctic coast which developed to become meeting places for tradesmen from Russia, Denmark/Norway, Sweden and elsewhere in western Europe. They were often called the "Lapp markets" as the Lapps (Sami) also met there, and their goods were in popular demand. Some of the markets were in the borderlands between Russia and Norway, e.g. in Karlebotn in Varanger, Kjørvåg (Aiddegoppe, Vaidaguba) on the Rybachiy Peninsula and at Kildin, just east of the Kolafjord. Once the English had reopened the sea route to the mouth of the Dvina in the 1550s and especially after Archangel was founded in 1584, sea trade between western Europe and Russia

expanded rapidly. But it seems that the North Norwegian traders did not travel further than to the nearest markets on the Russian side. We also have records of Russians visiting the Varanger market.

The established theory is that the Pomor trade did not start until around 1740. A source from 1744 records that Russian trading vessels had arrived in Vardø three years previously, at about the same time that Russian fishermen began fishing off Finnmark. It is, nevertheless, clear that Russian traders had already travelled along the coast of North Norway for many years. We hear of a Russian boat unloading goods in Tromsø in 1725, and several years previously Russians had visited Vannøya in North Troms. Before then they had been in Varanger. Already in the 1680s the tax collector in East Finnmark complained that the Russians traded in the fjord, and "Russian flour" was a well-known expression. It is said that, around 1690, the Russians sailed to Vardø and Vadsø twice a year with flour, grain, canvas and woven woollen cloth, axes, leather, wooden plates, spoons, etc. This trade went against the Danish-Norwegian monoploy regulations. However, even the government officials bartered with the Russians. One of the businessmen in Vadsø could even speak Russian and acted as host for the Russians while they lay in port.

It is thus possible to claim that the Pomor trade – the maritime-based Russian trade with North Norway – is older than previously considered. However, it is clear that it increased in volume and expanded geographically around the middle of the 1700s, a time

Pomor captain Sabortsjikoff. (Photo: Vardø Museum).

27

when it also drew much attention from the authorities.

The Pomors and free trade

In the 17th and 18th centuries, trade in North Norway was regulated by the prevailing commercial ideology, and most strictly in Finnmark. In 1681 all business was monopolized, first by the merchants in Bergen and later, after a brief spell of liberalization, by merchants in Copenhagen. But from the very beginning, there was opposition to this monopolization. The stirring of liberalism in western Europe and in Denmark-Norway cast a critical light on the system, and the Russians played a central role in the debate about the economic politics in the north. Although it was formally illegal, trade eastwards was permitted, especially when normal supplies failed or during years of famine such as the 1740s and 1770s. During years of trouble such as the Prussian Seven-years-war (1756–63), the authorities were more careful, however. In reality, trade with the Russians developed into a regular business, with Russian vessels making yearly visits to ports in Finnmark and Troms, especially after about 1760. Vardø and Vadsø became transit ports for Russian goods on their way westwards, and payment was often made in roubles. Lofoten and Vesterålen were sometimes visited, and Russian boats even turned up as far south as Salten. The good political relationships between Russia and Denmark-Norway during the second half of the 18th century contributed to this trade (and Russian fishing) being tolerated.

But the most important reason for the authorities wanting to regulate this trade more stringently was the claim by many local communities and officials that it was so economical and neccessary that it simply couldn't be stopped. The Russians exported many vital goods such as flour and grain which, in the beginning, were exchanged for leather goods and home industry products, such as woollen blankets, as well as factory products and foodstuffs. At this stage cod was not such an important product as it would be later; fish such as halibut and flounder were preferred. Furthermore, the Russians were not only considered as direct competitors with local merchants but, in an evaluation of the Pomor trade in a report on "Finnmark's development" in the 1780s, a radical proposal was put forward: the abolition of the monopoly system, free trade and the founding of market towns. The government followed this up with a decree in 1787 which allowed free trade from 1789, and the Russian trade was legalized in the market towns which were to be established in Troms and Finnmark as well as in the Finnmark trading stations. Thus the new economic ideology – based on liberal principles – was adopted in Denmark-Norway, with the north of the country acting as a "guinea pig". Trade with Russia had been the main incentive to start the process.

Rise and fall

During the first few years, it seems that business went very much by the book. This meant that the new town of Tromsø was the only market town in the county which profited by it. Furthermore, it was soon obvious that large quantities of goods were smuggled into the country, especially in Finnmark, and an increased liberalization was demanded. The first expansion came in 1796 when direct trade was permitted with the fishermen in Finnmark during the warmest part of the summer (when it is too warm to hang fish to dry). During the six weeks between 10 July and 20 August, they were allowed to sell fresh fish only. By this time, cod was increasing in importance as the main trading product. During the Napoleonic War in the early 1800s, the importance of this trade and especially the import of flour was emphasized. Despite the English blockade, North Norway had a steady supply of good Russian flour, especially via Eastern Finnmark. The trade law of 1830 not only extended the summer trade by two weeks, but also lifted some other regulations. But more significant was the 1839 act which allowed direct free trade also to Senja, Tromsø, Lofoten and Vesterålen.

Pomorship on the Dvina.

This expansion was naturally not only a result of the demands of the locals, but also reflected the general liberalization of trade and businesses in Norway throughout the 1800s. The fisheries in North Norway also increased tremendously in volume, especially after about 1840. This meant that exports to Russia were possible without any threat to the home market. In 1863 the summer season was expanded by yet another two weeks, and finally in 1874 to the period 15 June – 31 September. In 1863, export of salted fish was permitted, and the liberalization culminated in 1882, when the export of dried fish to Russia was also allowed.

The Pomor trade was based primarily on the bartering of goods, not buying and selling using money. This was almost inevitable because of the widespread subsistence economy of the region. The most valuable goods from Russia were difficult to come by in North Norway – flour, grain and building materials such as planks, timber and birch bark (for roofing). In addition, the Russians could supply

less essential but equally important products such as rope, ironware, leather and canvas. Cheap exotic products such as honey, sweets, nuts and brightly painted spoons and plates also helped brighten up the drudgery of daily life. Norwegian products were equally in demand in Russia. The Russians were not self-sufficient in fish, and religious fasts led to a great demand for fish at certain periods of the year. At one time the North Norwegian fishing industry was based nearly solely on the production of dried fish. However, the development of the trade eastwards meant that the fishermen could also extend their season into the warmer parts of the year when it was otherwise impossible to hang fish to dry because of flies. Cod and saithe were the main products delivered fresh to the Russians, who then salted them on board their ships. Salt thus also became an important export product from Norway, as did various foodstuffs, including tea, the Russian national beverage. The North Norwegian towns become important trading ports between western Europe and northern Russia. A curious pidgin language developed during the Pomor trade called "Russian-Norwegian".

The form of trade and business turnover changed in character during the 1800s. Although direct bartering never ceased, there was a tendency towards an increase

Loading timber cargoes in Archangel, ca 1910.

in buying and selling using cash and bills of exchange by the well-established merchants. But trade with the commoners remained a simple exchange of goods for goods, with the price of oatmeal as a common "monetary standard". The trend was for the less well-off Pomor skippers and merchants to travel up into the fjords and into less-populated areas while the richer skippers entered the towns and large fishing villages where they traded directly with Norwegian merchants and landowners. Some Russians were even granted credit by their Norwegian colleagues. They returned year after year, some for decades, and thereby built up mutual trust.

The Pomor fleet changed in character during the second half of the 1800s. The small Russian vessels (the *lodjer, kasmarer* and *ansiker*) were replaced by larger ketches and schooners. Many were bought in Norway, while others were built in the White Sea area. When a steamship service was started between North Russia and Finnmark in the 1870s, the steamships took over some of the freightage. One result of this was the so-called "cask-trade" in which Norwegian merchants salted fish in large casks which were then exported to Russia.

The true value of the Pomor trade is very difficult to quantify. Although customs duty should have been paid for the goods, much of the trade was unregistered. There are also huge discrepancies between the Russian and Norwegian customs declarations, and there is little doubt that the Pomors purposely tried to avoid paying duties at home. However, we do get some idea of the extent and development of the trade from the material available.

Around 1840, 350-400 Russian vessels entered ports in Troms and Finnmark. In 1870-1890, the average figure was about 290, ranging from 250-350. Numbers dropped during the early 1890s, only to increase again to about 300 in 1898. After the turn of the century, these figures become more difficult to estimate, as many vessels sailed twice a year while others spent the winter in Norway so that they could load up as

Russian coffee cups brought to Norway during the Pomor trade, (Photo: Tromsø Museum).

early as possible the following spring. The number of calls in port remained fairly high with over 200 in 1913. However, it seems that the number of vessels decreased, although the overall tonnage per vessel was by then much greater than it was in the middle of the 1800s.

The volume of trade varied from year to year in response to a variety of factors – the political situation, the corn harvest, the fisheries, and the international economy. It increased both in volume and value for both sides until the 1870s, when Russian exports stagnated before dropping slightly just before the First World War. The drop applied especially to oatmeal, which decreased sharply in volume in the 1890s. Norwegian exports to Russia increased rapidly and at the end of the 1870s exceeded the imports. In the 1890s, it was double the volume of Russian exports, six times higher in 1905 and eight times higher in 1912. At that time the value of Russian exports was about 2/3 of its value in the 1870s.

Trade came to an end for several reasons. First, its character changed from simple bartering to buying and selling. Second, each side's economy slowly became integrated in the respective national and international economies which resulted in, among other things, a more secure and cheaper source of imported corn from western markets. And third, the outbreak of the Great War and the change in the Russian regime in 1917 soon put a stop to trading. However, long before this, the Pomor trade had become a political issue in Norway.

"The locals love this trade"

Among the Norwegian attitudes to the trade, that of the local communities was almost unanimously positive, from start to finish. As a scholar reported from his travels in Finnmark, "The locals love this trade and show a unusual desire to fish so long as they can sell to the Russians". The Pomor trade was a source of income and goods at a time of year when Norwegian merchants did not otherwise buy fish. Furthermore, the Norwegians could negotiate a price for their fish directly with the Russians. The latter attempted to fix prices, but rarely succeeded. As the season drew on and the Russians wanted to get home, preferably fully laden, the price of flour generally fell. Each and every fisherman had one main goal, to ensure a supply of flour for the winter: "It was as if they came with bread for the winter". There is hardly any doubt that this trade gave the fishermen greater economic independence than they would otherwise have had trading with Norwegian suppliers and merchants. As spring approached, expectations rose. "The Russians" represented a life-saving supply of goods, as well as an exciting and colourful supplement to daily life. The signs were clear, as in the saying from Sør-Varanger: "With the spring fog come the Russians" – i.e. when the White Sea was again navigable.

"It should be encouraged rather than hindered"

The local governmental officials in the north were also positively disposed to the Pomor trade, and were even active in its liberalization. Thorkel Fjeldstad, the chief administration officer of Finnmark, wrote in 1775 that "from its importance, and I dare say neccessity, it should be encouraged rather than hindered". Corn products from Bergen had at that time become so expensive and supplies so short that many would have starved had they not had access to Russian corn and flour. This was especially true during times of crisis, such as during the Napoleonic Wars and the Crimean War (1853–56). Fjeldstad's opinion was representative of all the local officials throughout the 18th and most of the 19th centuries. A long series of his colleagues supported this trade and urged its expansion. Among them were Ole Hannibal Sommerfeldt, Ole Edvard Buck, and pastor and member of parliament P.V. Deinboll, who were succeeded by several MPs from the region. Buck wrote a very detailed report in 1842 from a study tour two years earlier in which he concluded that trade had developed in a "natural direction" without any administration from either country. From the Norwegian point of view, the Russian transport of the goods was advantageous in that North Norway did not have a fleet of boats which could handle this trade. The fleets which did exist had to concentrate on fishing and transporting local, coastal freight. The local administration, town boards and councils also defended the Pomor trade.

"An untimely competition"

But from the very start, the Pomor trade also had its opponents. During the 1700s, the members of the trade monopoly in Finnmark were very wary of the Russians. In the 1770s, representatives from the Copenhagen

List of goods delivered by a Pomor trader to merchant Chr. Figenschau, Helgø. (Photo: Tromsø Museum).

33

monopolists in Vadsø claimed that the Russians unfairly forced down the price of fish. The Bergen merchants fought tooth and nail against the liberalization of trade with the Russians as they claimed it would lead to their ruin. During the early phases of legalized trade, the local merchants were probably also against its expansion as they too feared a drop in business, and possibly also that the bond between the fishermen and their suppliers would slacken. But their opposition was not strong and no real competition developed as long as the trade was restricted to the summer months and to fresh fish. The local opposition appeared mostly in the form of anonymous newspaper articles which were strongly moralizing: "The people are being exploited by the Russians", "Norwegian trade is being threatened", etc. One thing is clear: these articles were not written by fishermen.

Towards the end of the 1800s, the Pomor trade became a political issue. This was due to the question of foreign policy concerning the "Russian danger", as well as a question of economics. Increased competition among buyers of fish and extensive Russian fishing off the Finnmark coast, with land bases in East Finnmark, were drawn into the debate. Opposition also arose when the sale of salted and dried fish was permitted, especially from the merchants outside

---

The Pomor captain Ikonnikoff and family. He traded in Tromsø for many years. (Photo: Tromsø Museum).

the realms of the Pomor trade, i.e. those based in southwestern parts of Norway who had a long tradition of trading with North Norway. They demanded that this "untimely competition" from the Russians should be prohibited. They gained some support from the government, who appointed a commission to propose a new trade law. The commission presented its proposal in 1897: dried cod should only be bought and sold by Norwegian citizens, and the Russians should be restricted to purchasing fish during the summer months.

This angered the fishermen. Apart from the whaling, the Pomor trade was the most important political issue in the region at the time. It led to the mobilization of the labour movement and resulted in the election of the first socialists to parliament during the 1903 elections, all of whom were from North Norway. Mass meetings of workers and fishermen, councils and MPs, partly supported by local merchants, all opposed the proposal. Their southern colleagues were not happy and accused them of selling themselves to a foreign nation for a mere handful of kroner.

After several years of intense debate, this trade law was passed in 1907. The result, or rather its interpretation, was that the fishermen were obliged to restrict their business with the Russians to the summer months. All other business was to be undertaken through Norwegian merchants who then could sell to the Pomors. During the following years, the law was much discussed, especially the practical affect it had on trade between the Russians and Norwegians. In reality, it probably meant little, but the locals' actions showed how important it was for the people of the region.

The end
The Pomor trade was, naturally enough, greatly reduced during the First World War. An attempt was made to revive it during the Allies' intervention in Russia in 1918, and the Tsar's fall did not put a stop to North Norwegian optimism. Some private individuals and firms even went so far as to buy roubles despite the drop in the exchange rate. This resulted in a series of bankruptcies, including that of the Finnmark Commercial Bank in 1920 with its piles of worthless roubles. The last fleet of Pomor vessels sailed in 1918, and until 1928 only single vessels arrived and left. But then the inevitable happened and the two hundred years of trade came to an end. Ships were abandoned and were left lying in port for years until they were broken up or rotted away.

It is often difficult to evaluate such a historic phenomenon, or rather the end of it. Even though it had long been recognized that the importance of the Pomor trade had diminished, few thought that it was of no importance. And its end did affect North Norway. First, there is little doubt that the trade had had a stabilizing influence on the local economy. Bartering helped the security and flexibility of household economies, and it is quite likely that the loss of the Pomor trade had serious consequences for the coastal Sami and their livelihood. For many, the change to a market economy and cash trade was sudden and difficult. Second, the collapse of Russia and its subsequent foreign curency problems and the collapse of the rouble that arose after the change in regime caused headaches for the local businesses and financial institutions. It probably also contributed to the economic dificulities experienced by many local municipalities during the next few decades. And finally, the end of the Pomor trade signified the end of a culture – with its linguistic element – which had developed over generations. North Norway became poorer, culturally as well as economically.

Einar Niemi,
Institute of Sosial Science,
University of Tromsø,
9037 Tromsø.

The drum, the shaman and the world – shamanism in the north

HARALD O. LINDBACH

The shaman and his drum are well-known symbols in arctic religions. But how similar are they and what is their relation to the Christianity?

It is quite normal to describe some religions as involving the worship of natural phenomena. It is said that some people pray to "stones and poles" or that they worship the sun–god or the wind–god. But this is only part of the truth. It's not the sun or the wind itself which is worshipped or ritualized, but the powers and forces which are manifested or felt when the sun shines or the wind blows. People don't believe in what they see, but in what lies behind what they see.

There are differences among religions in their attitudes to different cults or creeds. Some religions are open or "including" with respect to their ceremonies, or cult, but completely "excluding" when it comes to faith. Others, such as the ancient Sami religion or even the old Norse religion, were "including" with regards to faith, and allowed people to believe in almost anything they wished. But the cult was closed to all outsiders, not only strangers but also women and children.

The Norwegian church represented something completely different. Everyone was welcome to participate in the worship of God, but the creed was dictated from the pulpit. The encounter between Christianity and the Norse religion was a meeting of two ways of understanding one's existence. This is shown in the tactics St. Olav used on his missions. He knew that the old religion called on gods and powers that brought in good harvests and victory over enemies, but if stronger powers were presented as an alternative, the people would not be unwilling to try them instead.

If one could prove that there was a new and stronger power, it would not be difficult to persuade the people to believe in it. But such methods were useless a hundred years later when the Sami were to be converted. For them the church arrived with alien thoughts, unfamiliar ideas and little understanding of the Sami's culture, language and history. Furthermore, the Sami already knew a little about the church and

Christianity, and many had accepted some of the ideas which they found useful or necessary.

In the beginning, i.e. around year 1100 AD, Christianity as a religion was a new and alternative way of interpreting and understanding the truth. To some degree it could be combined with the beliefs that the Sami already held, even to the extent that, e.g., a picture of a church could be painted on their magic drum. Crucifixes have also been found in Sami sacrificial sites. In these early days, the Sami were open to the powers which the church stood for, but as time passed this openess cooled, and nothing "Christian" has been found in newer sacrificial sites. To begin with, Christianity was simply considered to be another religion, but later it became a hostile force: a view of reality belonging to the people in power. A bitterness grew among the Sami which was not always strong enough to result in action, but it was there.

Some researchers maintain that, for centuries and at least until the middle of the 1700s, the Sami practiced both Christianity and their old religion. They claim to have found many Christian concepts mixed with the heathen, i.e. Sami beliefs became more and more influenced by the West European mentality as time passed. This is probably true because, in religion, it is quite normal for ideas, rites and myths to be supplemented with new content. But painting a church on their ritual drum did not only mean that they were open to new ideas. It probably also signified that the noaiden's (the Sami sorcerer's) realm

Sibirian shaman. (Ratzel, 1895).

of power had expanded so that the Sami could safely enter the sphere of a different religion. We can see this in the advice given to those whose children were christened: once back home, the Christian blessing was to be washed off and the child given a new and better name.

What was the Sami religion, and what sources do we have? Let us look at the latter first.

There are numerous sources, both written and oral, passed down through the tradition of storytelling. We also have accounts from other arctic races with Euro–Asiatic connections, within which the Sami religion belongs. These written accounts are of varying quality as historic documents, with the author often recording what other people had seen or heard. The strange and mysterious elements are often emphasised, such as sorcery and gann.

Others, such as the missionaries of the 1700s, recorded what they saw or what they heard from the Sami themselves, but again with their own interpretations. Naturally enough, the Sami were not very willing to tell everything about their, or other people's religious practices to strangers who wouldn't understand much anyway. The danger and fear of being ridiculed and condemned were well founded. And could they be sure that they wouldn't be punished for their beliefs despite being promised otherwise? But most important of all, the revealing of cult secrets was a violation of their own religion. What would happen if one stepped outside the sphere in which the noaid's power was effective? Thomas Westen describes the terror experienced by those who had "confessed" or had told how they practiced their religion.

When referring to the various gods and spirits, there are three possible sources of error in the oldest written records. First, the pagan gods of the 1700s were considered to be the same as the gods of Antiquity, and this influenced both the questions asked by the missionaries and the answers received. Second, the answers were compared with the Christian rights and beliefs and considered as a devilish misrepresentation of Christianity. And third, the Sami gods were often

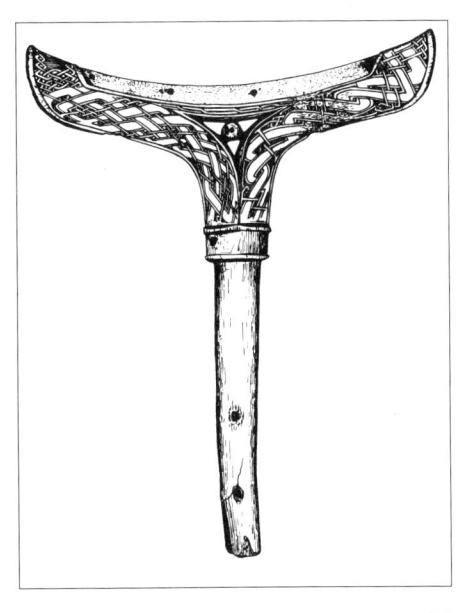

Hammer for a Sami shaman drum, found at Sørøya. (Photo: Tromsø Museum).

associated with the corresponding Norse gods, e.g. Thor Horagallis. This often makes it difficult to determine the names of the gods and how people understood them. Knud Leem discovered this in Porsanger when, in the 1750s, he found that the missionaries' list of gods did not tally with that of the locals. The Porsanger Sami had heard of some of those on his list, but not of the others. This was because many of the names on the list had been collected in the south of the country, and some of their creeds and beliefs were unknown in the north.

The drum

The drum was a medium through which the powers that influenced the outcome of the hunt, trapping and other important activities were contacted. They were summoned and revealed themselves through the drumming. The drum was used as a medicine for illnesses, a prophetic voice of luck or misfortune, and a voice to explain or interpret the wishes of the powers. To listen to the drum was like listening to the heartbeat of life. And life is indeed what was painted on the drum – figures which remind us of rock–carvings, symbols representing important stages between birth and death. A synopsis of the powers, people and animals was painted with alderbark dye on the drum head in a distinct pattern so that the noaid could understand what needed to be done or not done as the message was transmitted during the drumming. The message came not only from the voice of the drum, but also when the arpa moved over the symbols.

The arpa is a ring made of bone which moves over the drum head as it is beaten with a hammer of horn, bone or metal. Both the ring and the hammer are found among the people of Siberia. Although there are differences in the drums of, e.g., the Nganasan–sjaman and the Sami, one is struck more by the similarities than the differences in the drums found across the Arctic. The Sami drum head is nearly completely covered by symbols, but for others only half the head is covered, symbolizing both the visible and the invisible.

Outside the Sami region, we have documentation from, e.g., Nganasan showing how important drums were all across the Arctic. It seems that each

*Sami shaman – **noaid**. (Knud Leem, 1767).*

family had a drum and, in some cases, they were used as instruments of prophecy. They could be used alone or with others. But the drums also had a central role as instruments used in ceremonial songs and dances across the arctic nations.

How old is shamanism?
Among the stone–age rock–carvings at Skavberg on Kvaløya just outside Tromsø, a ritual drum is depicted . In other words, we can assume that drum beats have been heard over the Nordkalotten for as long as people have lived there. In addition it may be possible to trace West European shamanism behind witchcraft which was heavily persecuted. "Witchcraft" is based on local magic arts, themselves based on ancient forms of shamanistic religion.

Several years ago, an 18 cm long wooden pin was found in Oppdal. It is 7000 years old and is the oldest wooden artifact found in Norway to date. Its form is such that it could be interpreted as being a hammer for a shaman drum.

As already mentioned above, pictures are painted or drawn on drums in a different manner from place to place. There are four main types, distinguished by the pattern of the symbols on the head. They also differ in size, from about an arm's length in diameter to half that. The Tofa–shams, who live in the Sajan Mountains in Siberia, have large round drums and beat them with a spade–shaped drumstick made of bone, horn or wood. Hanging round the rim are small wooden sculptures and amulets. Attached to the Nganasan drums are long, pencil–thick wooden figures of, e.g. reindeer or weasels. They are interpreted as being the shaman's helpers.

The noaid/shaman
The expressions "shaman" and "shamanism" were used to avoid using words such as "wizard", "medicine–man" or "conjurer". Shamanism is at least as old as the rock–carvings which themselves tell us much about the rituals where the shaman acts to ensure a good hunt. The Ojibwa Indians in Canada drew a picture before the hunt and sang a prayer to assure a successful hunt. This same ritual combination of the drawing, the song and the shaman turns up again in hunting scenes in southern Norway and in Siberia. Shaman songs are known from many indigenous races, including the Evenki.

However, shamanism is not so uniform that one can talk about a well–defined pattern of faith and ideas. Much, if not most, is no more than guesswork. Nevertheless, we are fairly certain that there is some connection between the religions of the arctic peoples, and these religions date back so far that we can use shamanism to explain many of the signs in the hunters' art. One expert has described several human–like figures that show men and women in situations which have nothing to do with daily life: there are "puppets" and "skeletons", there are pixie– like dancing figures on the wall of the cave Solsemhulen in Leka, Nord–Trøndelag, and there are "symbol–carriers" at Namsfors in Sweden. They depict cultic situations where the shaman tried to contact the "other" world, the invisible world.

Who could become a shaman?
It seems that the position of shaman was hereditary. In many cases among the arctic peoples, we find a pattern within particular shaman families with a clear case of shamans coming from a single family such that there was one in nearly every generation. But being a shaman was also a question of talent. If we look at the process of becoming a shaman, we find that there is something that matures in a person under some form of pressure.

A.A. Popov relates how a Nganasan Samojed became a shaman. The shaman had to be descended from a shaman, and he had to have the neccessary skills. The ritual involved a person clothed in black and white appearing before the Ngangasan and asking a series of questions to which he had to guess the answers: that the clothes should be made of seven reindeer skins, that the drum should be made of three, and that a wild male reindeer would show him which reindeer should be sacrificed and skinned. "You will be a powerful shaman", says the man. But that is not the wish of the Ngangasan. Then he sees seven moon– like figures of copper (which have healing properties) and nine human figures of iron, and these apparitions show that he was indeed to be a shaman. He also sees iron and copper from which to make amulets, and he starts to look for the right tree from which to form his drum. He finds it in the end. "Come", says the tree, "I am for you".

The Samojeds divide the shamans into several groups. First there is the mighty shaman, who is very wize and can perform miracles, then come the less powerful ones with fewer capabilities. In addition there are good and evil shamans. The Nenets call the lowest ranking shamans the "dream–seers" or "seers", and the Selkup Samojeds have a true shaman who can mediate contact between humans and the spiritual world. The shaman is nearly always a man. Female shamans were not usual west of

Solon-Mongol shaman. (Nationalmuseet).

the river Jenisej, but were common among the Evenki people. Both men and women could tell fortunes, heal, etc., but very few could reach the level of shaman. A old Tofa–shaman related, "I was only a little shaman with seven spirits. Others were much bigger, with up to 27 spirits".

But to become a shaman wasn't only a question of ancestory and talent. The most talented often trained under an older shaman for a long time. Training was neccessary to be able to carry out all the tasks and to faithfully pass on the traditions. Ancient knowledge concerning healing, the weather, planets, hunting and trapping needed to be aquired, songs learnt, and even a special shaman language had to be used in cult rituals. An expert not only sang songs he had learnt, but also composed his own.

Siberian sources tell us quite a lot about the dress and equipment a shaman used. The frame of the drum was tightened in a special way, and the costume sewn in a special pattern. Furthermore, the headdress was of a particular type of skin. But there were, of course, variations. The Ngangasan shaman had a helmet with a visor, probably to block his vision so he could concentrate when he entered a trance. The Tofas had their own special type of shoe. It is said that when the shaman put on these special clothes, they entered another sphere.

What was expected of the shaman?
1. He was a healer, and had insights into the nature of illnesses, and how they could be cured.
2. The shaman led the neccessary rituals before the hunt.
3. The shaman could tell fortunes. He could interpret dreams and when neccessary, enter a trance. He also had telekinetic and telepathic powers.
4. He conducted ceremonies to ward off the unwanted and to encourage that which was desired. He also carried out ceremonies for the dead.
5. The shaman was an adviser and could gather information about what the powers wanted
6. He led sacrificial acts.

The world and the powers
Kai Donner (1913) relates that along the River Ket, each small group of people had its mediator between the people and the powers. Every evening one could hear drums beating and the shaman singing in nearly every tent. Songs about the shaman's achievements, successful hunts, happiness and sorrows were sung. The shaman also told stories and maintained the traditions concerning all the spirits, gods and powers that ruled in the forests, mountains and plains. Much of this was expressed in such a poetic and fanciful language that it was impossible to understand it all. Some powers couldn't be named, and others could not be portrayed. One such was the nature god of the Samojeds. He was especially unpredictable and had to be placated with sacrifices, or chastised with heat.

The shaman also sings on his way to the land of the spirits, having first become intoxicated by eating fly agaric. He is otherwise fit and healthy. Before the ritual begins, all dogs are banished from the tent. Then the shaman yawns, puts on his headdress and sleeps for a while. When he wakes up he has become someone else with a different voice. He then starts drumming while calling for his assistants and singing. Parts of the song are repeated by the others in the tent. The song concerns the difficulties which arise during his "journey", and gradually he comes to understand the conditions which need to be fulfilled. He promises that there will be sacrifices and that he will give his soul as security for this to happen. He may take someone's knife and scratch himself. After his conversation with the spirits, his "return" begins with a prayer of release and then a long sleep. There is much dancing during his return.

Relationships to plants and animals
A priest in Narym in western Siberia wrote in about 1910 that some of the people there were supporters of totemism, and thought that humans were descended from animals.

There are signs of totemism all over the Arctic, in that there is always a close relationship between humans, animals, birds and plants. A flower has a "soul" just like humans, and there is, deep down, a relationship between everything that lives. The slaughtering of an animal is not considered destructive. Quite the opposite, it is the correct way to ensure the continuation of life. An animal sacrifice is something positive. Isak Olsen (1710) tells that the Sami left the sacrificial site in happiness and song. At the same time, the attitude to the victim was characterized by a mixture of feelings: joy, honour and fear. The sacrifices and rituals tell of a close

Female chakkar Mongol shaman. (Photo: Haslund-Christensen, 1939).

relationship between the hunter and the hunted. But the ceremonial actions were not only encouraged or discouraged things to happen. They also brought people together, and the rituals during the sacrifice had clear social dimensions. That which was expressed verbally through song, recitals, rituals and drumbeating, together with the ritual meals, underlined the sense of solidarity. When the animals killed during the hunt were brought home, they were often received and shared in a ritualized manner. A seal caught by the Inuits on Perry Island in Alaska was divided up according to a predefined pattern. Two of the hunters were "lung partners" and received the lungs, two were "heart partners" or "rib partners" etc. One couldn't simply eat what one killed or found. It had to be divided properly, and handled in such a way that the relationships between beings were not disturbed.

Shaman with a drum and his helper. (Photo: Haslund-Christensen, 1936).

Women and the hunt

When the world is such that there is a bond between everything that lives, then there must be a special logic behind all actions. It is, for example, logical that the eagle, squirrel, elk, pine tree and plants that grow in a pine forest have common bonds. The eagle builds its nest in the trees, the squirrels live in them, the elk eats the plants, etc.

The bear and especially the elk are depicted in the hunting art of the rock–carvings in North Norway, but their bones are hardly ever found in archaeological excavations. This is probably because they were well hidden after the animal was slaughtered. It is well known that skeletons and bones of some animals are handled in a special way, e.g. from the Bible, Exodus 12, verse 46: "You shall not carry forth any of the flesh outside the house; and you shall not break a bone of it". Another story involves Thor and the goat he slaughtered. The bones were wrapped in the skin and when Thor lifted his hammer, the goat came to life again. These animals have a special place in the relationship between humans, nature and the powers. After eating the flesh, all bones were treated in such a way that nothing was damaged, and we know of several cases where the bones of a bear were buried. This was to ensure both the success of future hunts and the reincarnation of the bear.

But how were man and the animals related? We can mention some of the patterns we know from Indian tribes in North America: there, eagles and humans hunt hares, thrushes and humans eat berries, bear and humans catch salmon, etc. It is easy to visualize a type of relationship between man and animals other than that seen by most humans today!

Women are somewhat autonomous in this connection. Normally they can not take part in the rituals during the sacrifice, but there are also some rituals and offerings which only women can perform. Women do not take part in the hunt, but if the hunt is to succeed, women need to be active both before and afterwards. A central part of the ritual performed when the carcass of a bear is brought home involves the preventive actions of the women. They chew and spit alder bark at the men in an attempt to rescue them from any dangerous situation they may be in after the hunt. But during this ritual, the women themselves are in danger and must cover their faces so as not to be recognized by the bear. For instance, the Samojed women drew a ring of soot round their eyes and on their right cheek when they cooked bear meat. Because everyone was in danger, the bear was brought in through the back of the tent. Similar rituals are carried out by the Nivkhi tribe on Sakhalin in Siberia. There is clearly such a close relationship between bears and man that the hunt, eating, etc. becomes a very complicated process. The fact that the bear is often called "father", "old man", etc. over the whole of northern Europe is just a of this.

The alder tree, woman and bears are connected in a strange way, and the various forces between them can be transferred or neutralized. Or perhaps we can say that women can transfer these dangerous forces to one or another essential life process because they are closest to plants and animals. They give birth and thereby carry life onwards. As Ante Pirak writes, "I have even heard that bear blood was called "leipe", the same word as is used today for women's menstrual blood". And when we find that the Sami word for alder is "leaibi", we can see this relationship yet again. But this is just one of many such connections. Others occur between stars and plants, man, fish, birds and animals, trees and plants, etc.

Two mistakes we shouldn't make when talking about shamanism.
First, there is no reason to suppose we are dealing with a belief system in which doubt does not exist. Where there is belief, there is also doubt. Castren (ca. 1850) tried to ask the Samojeds about their beliefs about life after death. Only one answered, telling him: "You live like dogs, you rot where you rot". And when asked where the soul goes, he was told, "Go and see. Then you will find out". Or as Kai Donner (1921) was told, "I know about death. I've been there". He was told this by someone who had been delirious with fever and had seen the underworld.

As for the others: if something appears simple or naive, simpler that than we assume, then there is reason to believe that we don't understand it. The shamanistic people were very knowledgeable about health, about human relations, about their relationship with nature and how much mankind could harvest nature – no more, no less.

Harald O. Lindbach, Skillvassbakk, 8276 Ulvsvåg.

The Sami on the Kola Peninsula

HANS-ERIK RASMUSSEN

In common with many other peoples, the Sami are divided among several nations. Of the approximately 50,000 Sami, 30,000 today live in Norway, 15,000 in Sweden, 4,000 in Finland and 2,000 in Russia. As far as the Sami are concerned, the national borders are illusory, especially since they have been moved to and fro in the past. The Sami culture and language are common across the borders.

The Sami language can be divided into nine main dialects, of which two, the Kildin Sami and the Ter Sami, are spoken on the Kola Peninsula. During the 1979 census, 53% of the Sami defined Sami as their mother tongue. In Norway, 60% of the Sami have Sami as their mother tongue, and in Finland and Sweden the figure is about 50%.

Sami settlements on the Kola Peninsula
Most of the Sami are today concentrated on the tundra regions in the interior of the peninsula. Traditionally their settlements were spread across the whole peninsula even though the southern part was also settled by the Russians in the 1700s.

During the last century, and up to the the early 1900s, the Sami settlements were organized through each family's use of a territory for hunting, fishing and reindeer husbandry. This form of organization is called a siida (in Russian, pogost) and often consisted of winter quarters, plus spring and summer areas, depending on the source of living. Members of the siida identified themselves with the landscape: lakes, rivers, forests, stretches of coastline, etc. and each siida area was recognized as a "homeland". A series of political and economic factors have, however, radically changed this traditional form of settlement.

The establishment of the city of Murmansk in 1915, and the building of the Murmansk railway in 1915–17 forced the Kildin Sami eastwards and off much of their grazing lands. When the Finland/Soviet border was adjusted after the First World War, the Suenjel Sami's winter and summer lands were separated by the new border. The Suenjel siida has since moved west to Finland and are now settled north of Lake Inari (Sevettijärvi). After the Second World War and yet another border adjustment, the Petchenga Sami were also forced to settle in Finland, southeast of Lake Inari.

The establishment of non–Sami towns further intruded upon the siida territories, and they were often built in localities other than those where the traditional winter settlements existed. This applies to towns such as Petsamo/Petchenga, and Kola in the Kildin siida territory. Other siidas in western Kola had their territories flooded by hydro–electric schemes, and the Sami were forced to move further inland. Finally, some of the siidas were disbanded as a result of the Soviet establishment of the collectives for reindeer husbandry and fishing. In their place, towns such as Krasnostjelje (1921) and Kanevka (1923) were built.

The Sami were traditionally hunters and fishermen
The establishment of new settlements were not the only changes registered during the last century. The Sami lifestyle also changed considerably. Before the Soviet powers became influencial, the Sami did not have a uniform way of living. Some of the siida lived by hunting and fishing, others by keeping reindeer, and others were more seasonally determined. Within each siida there could also be large social differences. Some families did not own reindeer and were employed by those that did. These differences were the source of social dependence between individuals and families. Right up until 1927, there were some Sami families in the tundra interior who owned large reindeer herds. These herds could number 500–1,000 animals, while the majority of families only had a hundred or so.

Sami men in Lovozero, 1910. (Photo: Gustaf Hallstrøm).

At the end of the 1800s, a typical siida was characterized by a mixed economy (hunting, fishing, trapping), and each family may have had a couple of tame reindeer to pull sledges. It wasat this time that they started to tame reindeer on a larger scale, probably in order to increase their supply of food as the numbers of wild reindeer declined. But numbers were still limited to small herds of 20–30 animals. The large–scale Sami reindeer domestication on the Kola Peninsula is thus not an age–old tradition. It was, however, extensive in that the reindeer ran wild most of the year and were only herded for slaughtering, etc.

Other ethnic groups appear
In 1887, the situation changed dramatically. Huge herds of about 5,000 reindeer were driven into the siida areas from Siberia and competed for grazing lands. They belonged to the Komi who had been forced to move from their homelands along the banks of the river Izhma, west of the Urals, probably as a result of an epidemic outbreak which threatened their reindeer. With them they brought a very different, intensive herding culture. They also brought Nentsy along as herdsmen.

The Komi have since been a very dominating ethic group, both culturally and socially. The Izhma– Komi developed their form of reindeer husbandry in the 17th and 18th centuries but, in contrast to the neighbouring Nentsy, the Komi were not nomads. They lived in permanent settlements and

Sami women in Lovozero, 1910. (Photo: Gustaf Hallstrøm).

employed herdsmen, usually Nentsy. As a result, they also influenced the Nentsy culture (language and lifestyle). After the arrival of the Komi on Kola, the social and economic differences between the tribes increased. The Komi were generally the richest, and had large reindeer herds which were protected by Nenetsy and Sami herdsmen. As late as 1920, the town of Lovosero was divided into ethnic "quarters" with the Sami and Nenetsy living in one part, the Komi in the other – the latter often in larger and better–kept houses. The Sami culture (clothing, forms of transport, etc.) was thus also influenced by the Komi.

The old, ecologically balanced Sami mixed economy became overrun by the space–demanding, economically more sound and intensive form of reindeer herding. This situation was also paralelled in Sweden, where the intensive Sami nomadic way of life which was based solely on reindeer in the 1600s spread into regions with a mixed economy. However, on the Kola Peninsula, several ethnic groups were involved, increasing the levels of economic and social conflict.

Collectivization

After 1928, the collectivization of the private reindeer enterprises began. Again the different ethnic groups were to play decisive roles in that formal political power and economic bases varied among the groups. In this period, the Russians

---

Nenets women in Lovozero, 1910. (Photo: Gustav Hallstrøm).

made up the majority on the party organizations while the richest reindeer owners were mostly Komi. To start with, most effort was put into organizing of the poorest reindeer herders into collective farms, and withdrawal of more and more individuals and families out of private reindeer ownership.

The first Sami cooperative was established in 1928, and two reindeer breeding farms were established in Lovosero in 1929 – one Sami ("The Sami") and one Komi ("The reindeer watcher"). Several cooperatives were established throughout the peninsula in the early 1930s, but many of them failed due to bad and unqualified leadership. Several families even continued the traditional siida– system and moved out from the winter settlements in the spring. Furthermore, some of the last ones to be established contained a mixture of ethnic groups, which also caused problems.

The forced collectivization process in the early 1930s faced a lot of opposition throughout the Soviet Union. On farms thousands of animals were slaughtered in protest. The same applied to the reindeer areas. On the Kola Peninsula, the rich Komi reindeer owners actively slaughtered their reindeer and left them out on the tundra.

Area used by the Sami on the Kola Peninsula. (Rasmussen, 1990).

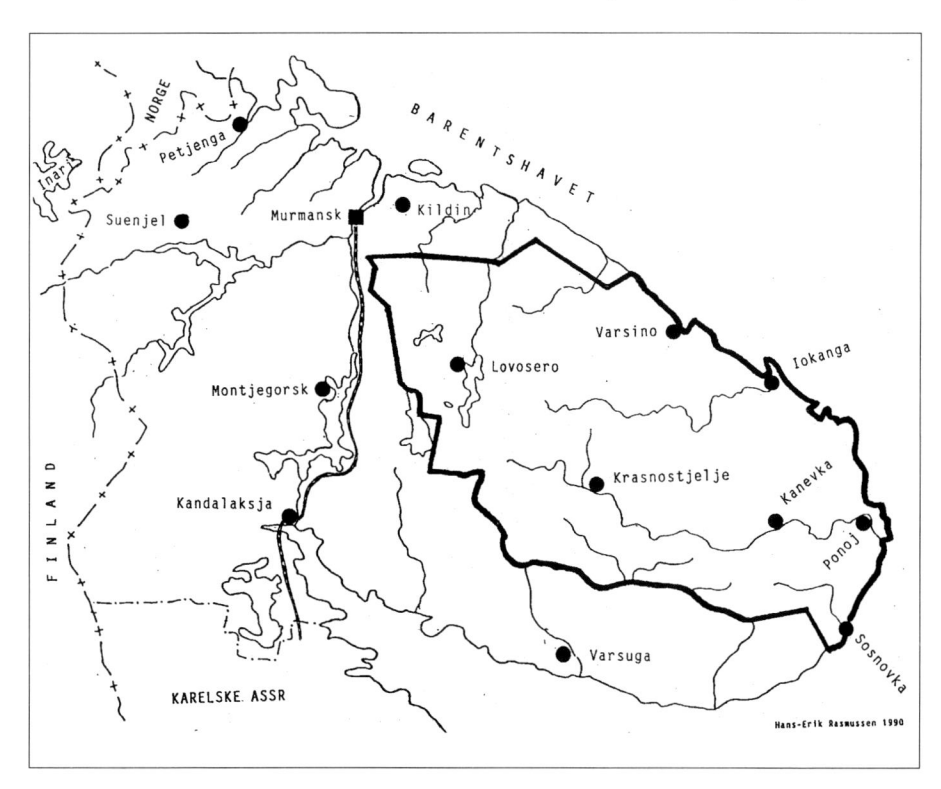

Collectivization in the Arctic regions was, however, slow. In 1931, only 12% of the households were in collectives; in 1934, 36% (who owned 10% of the reindeer); in 1940, 75% and in 1948, 97%. In comparison, over half of the Kola reindeer herders were collectivized by 1932.

In the middle of the 1930s, there was extensive regulation of the grazing areas, trek routes, calving areas, fishing lakes, etc. as part of the collectivization process. This resulted in the demise of the siida system, and the old siidas exist today only as reference points used by the Sami themselves. With the new land and water divisions, the earlier movement routes were shortened and the distances between the summer and winter areas were often halved (from e.g. 500 km to ca. 200 km). Permanent slaughter sites were established, and veterinary services were offered. In retrospect, one could say that the economics of the reindeer enterprizes were actually improved through this process.

The people and settlements

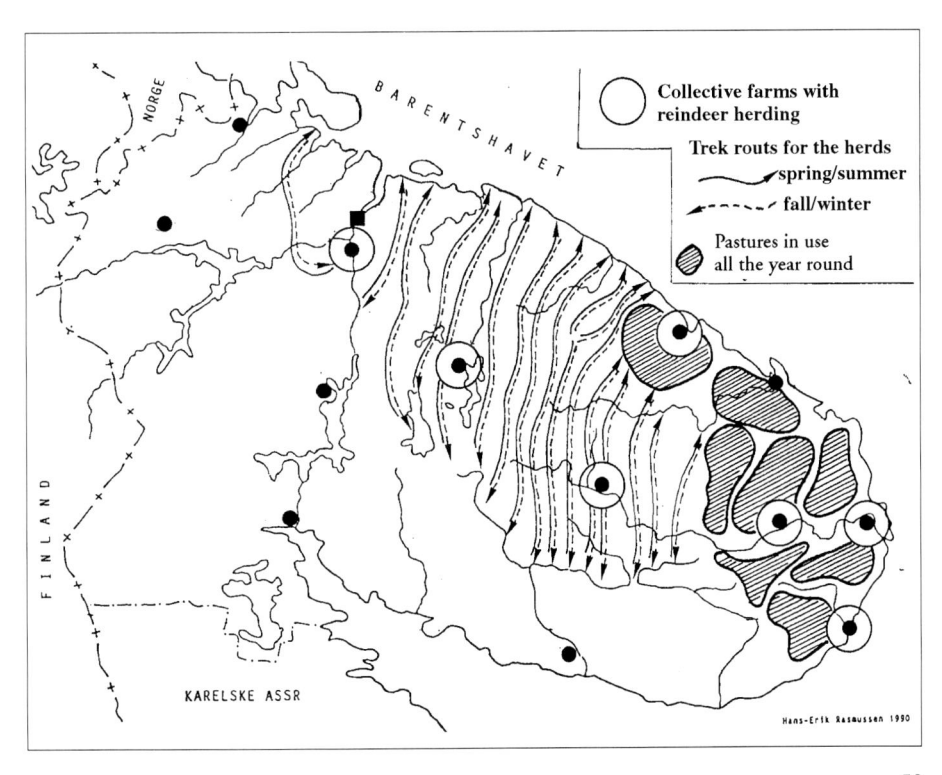

Besides a change in the type of reindeer enterprizes, there was a considerable centralization of the population on the Kola peninsula. Several of the collectives were disbanded or consolidated, while others were transformed to state farms (sovkhos). On the state farms, the workers were employed as paid hands, and in Lovozero, the reindeer herders are now organized on the state farm "Tundra".

The populations in the towns increased considerably after the 1950s, mainly due to immigration from other parts of the USSR. In 1959, the town populations constituted 51% of Murmanskaja Oblast (Murmansk Region). By 1989, this had increased to 92% with 99,000 people living outside the towns.

The relative populations of the ethnic groups on the Kola Peninsula have, however, remained nearly constant. The peninsula's population is made up of the following groups, listed in order of size: Russians, Ukranians, White Russians, Karels, Sami, Komi and Nenetsy. The Russian population constitutes 80–90% of the peninsula's population. The Sami number about 2,000.

According to the latest information, nearly 70% of the Sami men under 40 years old who live in Lovozero are single. Sami women have taken to marrying Russians and Komi and, whereas the Sami men continue with their reindeer, many of the Sami women leave the tundra to continue their education. They rarely return home. This has resulted in a shortage of Sami workers on the state farm "Tundra" in Lovozero, and the farm has to fetch workers from other regions and from other ethnic groups.

A new Sami organization

Towards the end of 1989, the Kola Sami

Migrating Sami in the Ter area, Kola Peninsula 1928. (Photo: Charnolusky, Russian Ethnographical Museum, St. Petersburg).

Organization was established. The first leader was Vasili Selivanov, and the organization is "an independent official organization which shall work for the social and economic development of the Sami minority, and preserve the Sami traditions based on harmony between the people and the environment. The organization shall further study and develop the Sami cultural heritage." The organization has nominated committees which consider topics such as language and education, social and economic questions, health, literature and environmental protection.

A number of the smaller administrative regions were disbanded during the Stalin period. It now seems that several "national regions" are now being re–established, and the new Sami organization is promoting the establishment of a special Sami region.

Hydro-electric schemes at Iokanga

The official Russian estimates of the expected energy demands show that the Kola Peninsula will be short of 1 billion killowatt hours in 1995. Plans for a new hydro–electric scheme along the Iokanga river have thus been drawn up.

Sami leaders have pointed out that the implementation of the plan will have far– reaching consequences. To start with, a large grazing area will be flooded. But more serious are the new roads and power lines which will be built across the tundra, straight through important reindeer districts. The power will supply the urban and industrial areas in the western part of the peninsula. Finally, a new town housing 10,000 construction and electricity workers will be built and will devastate an ecologically sensitive reindeer district.

Reindeer husbandry is the main source of living for the Sami people in Russia. The herders are one of the few – if not the only – groups who use the Sami language. An ecological threat to the reindeer is thus also a threat to the foremost Sami cultural values.

**Hans Erik Rasmussen,
Dept. of Eskimology,
University of Copenhagen,
DK-1401 Copenhagen K,
Denmark.**

The Russian Sami of today

LEIF RANTALA

What is the situation for the Sami on the Kola Peninsula today? How much contact have they had with the Scandinavian Sami, and how are they treated politically and economically?

This article is based on my own contact with the Kola Sami, which started when the first Russian Sami attended the 12th Sami Conference in Utsjoki in August 1983.

Contact between the Russian and Scandinavian Sami

Throughout the Soviet period, contact between the Kola Sami and the Sami in the west was extremely sporadic. In 1920, some of the Russian Sami ended up on the Finnish side of the border as a result of Finland annexing the Petsam region under the treaty of Dorpat. Fate had it that some of the families became split, with members on each side of the border, and they were not to meet again until 50 years later. The first contacts across the border after the October Revolution started in 1960, when a group of Norwegian southern Sami visited Lovozero. An article in the magazine Reindriftsblad (No.2/1960) is interesting in this context: its headline is "The Russians are way ahead of us in reindeer husbandry. Their industry receives more aid than ours".

In the 1970s, the Swedish Sami Paul Anders Simma visited Lovozero and wrote a short piece about the Russian Sami in the book Sámit-Samerna-Nordkalottensfolk edited by Boris Ersson and Birgitta Hedin. For most people, it was virtually impossible to get permission to visit Lovozero. Contact in the other direction was also difficult. The Russian Sami were invited to every Sami Conference in the 1960s and 1970s, but none ever attended. However, in the early 1980s the first signs of an opening appeared when the Russian Sami dance group Lujavr was allowed to visit Finland on several occasions. Then, to everyone's surprise, the first Russian attendee, Vasilij Selivanov turned up "as scared as a hare" (as he later told me) at the 12th Sami Conference held at Utsjoki in Finland. Since then, contact has been easier and easier, and in 1992 the Kola Sami could elect representatives to the Nordic Sami Council, resulting in a change of name to simply the Sami Council.

How the Kola Sami were organized

Towards the end of the 1980s, the Samis in Scandinavia started enquiries about when the Russian Sami would establish a Sami organization. This culminated in the foundation of the Associacija Kolskih Saamov (Association of the Kola Sami) in Murmansk on the 3rd of

September, 1989. The first chairman was Vasilij Selivanov, but he was soon succeeded by Nina Afanasjeva. The association has its head office in Murmansk and local branches in all towns where there are Sami, as well as in St. Petersburg.

In 1993, Kola Sami craftsworkers and arstists formed an organization, led by Anastasija Mozolevskaja. In 1994, a Sami youth organization, Saam Nurash, was formed, led by Maksim Filippov. The Sami womens' organization, Sáráhkka, has local branches on the Kola Peninsula and the Sami Council committees hold meetings of the Russian Sami leaders.

The Kola Sami took part in the foundation of an organization for the so-called minority groups in Northern Russia. Gorbatjov attended the first meeting in Moscow, as did several Scandinavian Sami. Yeremej Aipin, a Khant, is the chairman today, and the headquarters are in Moscow. The term "minorities of the north" is an official legal expression and includes 26 different minority groups spread between the Kola Peninsula to the west and the Bering Strait to the east. It should be noted that the Komi and Jakut are not included here. It is also most ironical that two of the poorest minority groups in Russia have relations in the west: the Sami and the Inuits.

The Scandinavian Sami have undoubtedly been a source of inspiration for the Russian Sami to organize themselves. The Russians have had models to follow, and the next stage will be to form a Sami Parliament on the Russian side as well. Work has started, but how long it will take is uncertain.

Sami settcement on the Muvman coast, western part of Kola, 1928. (Photo: Charnolusky, Russian Ethnographical Museum, St. Petersburg).

The Governor of the Murmansk region, Evgenij Komaraov, has let it be known that the regional administration is against the election of such a parliament.

The political and economical situation on the Kola Peninsula

Most of the Russian Sami live in the Lovozero county. Of a total population of about 18,000, 915 are Sami. Of the 3,500 who live in the county town of the same name, 20% are Sami. I thus choose this county (rayon in Russian) as an example of the political and economic situation for the Russian Sami.

The Sami had only three of the 55 seats in the Lovozero county authority which tells us something of their political influence, or lack of it, at the local level. The press, i.e. the Lovozerskaja Pravda, has repeatedly written about the seriousness of the situation, but has been in a constant battle for freedom of speech and truth (*pravda* in Russian). Many of the authorities, e.g. the military, the fire brigade, and the taxmen, use their power to supress the local population, and the new laws are often so badly written that people easily fall on the wrong side of them. One Sami craftsman tells that if she reports all her income to the authorities, 90% of her earnings are taken in tax.

The economic situation in Lovozero is catastrophic. According to the head of the labour office, Nikolaj Brylov, unemployment is as high as 60%. From a Scandinavian point of view, it seems strange that anyone can survive, although the inhabitants of Lovozero have fewer difficulties than those living in big cities. They can at least catch fish, pick berries and mushrooms and many of the Sami have contact with reindeer owners who supply them with a little meat. Worst off are the pensioners, the invalids and

Sami folk dance in Lovozero. (Photo: Leif Rantala).

others who have no possibility of getting out to fish or pick berries. Furthermore, the number of places one can fish is limited, as are the number of licences.

Tourism
When Lovozero was opened for westerners several years ago, the Sami and many others imagined rich foreign tourists would start streaming into the district. But this was not to be. After the first rush, the numbers have dropped. The Sami started about 15 different schemes, some of which are connected to tourism. However, the results have been disappointing. When they attempted to arrange fishing trips to the salmon river Ponoj, they came into conflict with a Finnish/American business.

Long and poor roads to Lovozero, the crime rate, a bad hotel and next to no restaurants don't help attract tourists. It's a pity, because Lovozero has a lot to offer. The museum is one of the best in Sameland, a cultural center has recently opened, and above all the hospitality of the Lovozero Sami is overwhelming – and anyone who is interested in the Sami is made to feel particularly welcome.

Culture
Much has degenerated on the Kola Peninsula, but one aspect has made advances: cultural activity. I have been visiting the Kola region since 1984 and have been able to observe a strong and rapid improvement in the culture. Ten years ago, there was one Sami group of singers, the Lujavr, which had published a Sami ABC-book, and there was a

Numbers of Sami in relation to Sami speakers in different areas on the Kola peninsula.

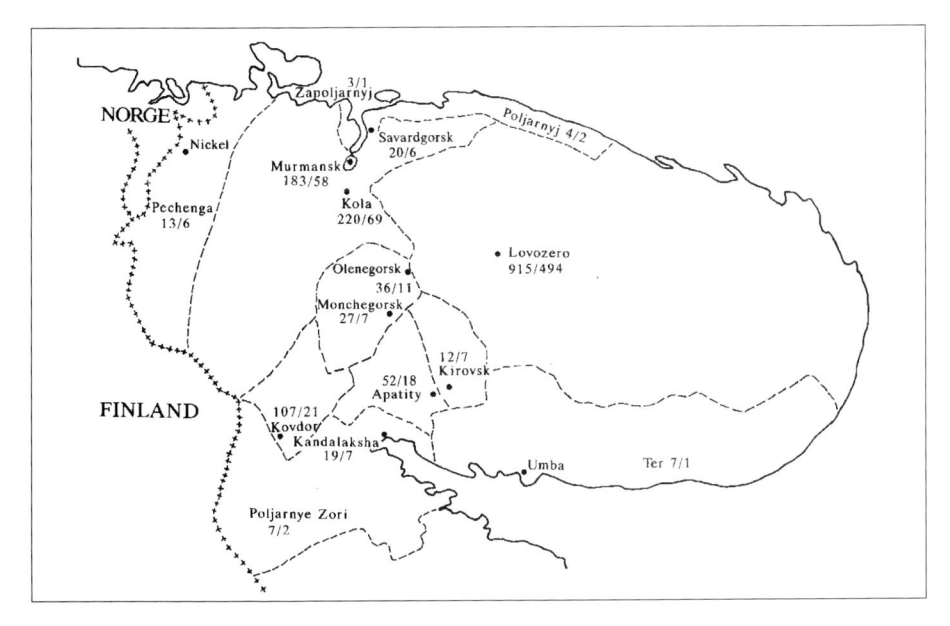

single comprehensive collection of Sami and Russian lyrics. Sami craftsmanship existed only in museums.

Today there are three groups of Sami dancers and singers, several collections of poems have been published in Sami, there are Sami broadcasts (40 minutes a week), and several Sami dictionaries have been published. In schools, about 30 textbooks in Sami are available, Sami is being taught in the boarding school in Lovozero, and courses in northern Sami are arranged. Karasjok, the Sami settlement in Finnmark which has a friendship bond with Lovozero, has been especially active in this field. The Sami Council has also given economic support to the cultural activities of the Kola Sami organizations, the various culture groups and to private individuals. The Sami Council has also initiated an aid scheme for the Russian Sami.

Craftsmanship is perhaps the cultural branch which has developed fastest. The Kola Sami had forgotten many of their traditional crafts, for instance no one could make the traditional woman's headgear any longer. To help out, the Scandinavian Sami arranged a series of craft courses for the Kola Sami in Lovozero and in Scandinavia, and whereas it used to be difficult to find Sami crafts on the Kola Peninsula, there is now a lot on offer in Lovozero.

Reindeer herding
There are about 70,000 tame reindeer on the Kola Peninsula, and several thousand wild ones. Most of them have belonged to the two "state farms", "Tundra" and "Lenin's Memorial". Earlier, reindeer herders were allowed to keep 35 animals for their own use. "Tundra" has been privatized, at least on paper. A steering committee consisting of reindeer herders

A typical log house in Lovozero. (Photo: Leif Rantala).

headed by Olga Anufrieva, a Sami, has been elected. The actual husbandry has hardly changed character, apart from very recently when a Swedish company, Nordfrys, started buying reindeer meat from Lovozero. They have even established their own slaughterhouse in Lovozero.

The company "Tundra" has had two or three years with economic problems, but now Swedish capital has recently saved it from the most pressing difficulties. However, a second problem has arisen in that there is now a shortage of reindeer meat in Lovozero because most of the production is now sent to Sweden.

A few Sami families have started farming reindeer privately with a few hundred animals each. They live in Loparskaja, about 40 kilometers south of Murmansk. Several of the Kola Sami have visited Scandinavia to study the reindeer business but, as in Scandinavia, only a small minority of the Sami on the Kola Peninsula own reindeer.

The reindeer owners on the Kola Peninsula have no organization to protect their rights. The biggest threat is

A unique photographe of Samis from five different countries: From the left: Tarja Porsanger, Utsjoki, SF, Lloyd Binder, Inuvik, Canada, Nina Afanasjeva, Murmansk, Peder A. Persen, Lakselv. Sitting: Lars-Anders Baer, Jokkmokk. (Photo: Leif Rantala).

poaching, and some reindeer owners have not only been threatened but also shot at by poachers.

What prospects do the Kola Sami have? Sadly, alcohol has become an integrated part of many of the Kola Sami lives and has resulted in endless misery for them. The mean life expectancy of a male Sami is only 44 years, slightly more for the women.

The Sami's future depends totally on Russia's future. It is true that the shops do have goods on their shelves, but few Sami can afford to buy them. And worse still is the energy situation. The houses in Lovozero are heated from a communal boiler which is fired using a type of oil called *mazut*. But because the inhabitants have no income, the council receives no taxes and thus has no money to buy the mazut. As a result, there have been long periods when the heating has been all but turned off and indoor temperatures have dropped down to 4-5^{0}C. Russian houses are so poorly built that they use eight times the energy needed to heat, e.g., Scandinavian houses. The Scandinavian Sami have tried to help those in the east. Humanitarian help has been sent across the border, collaborative projects have been started, language and crafts courses have been initiated, grants have been given to Russian Sami scientists and to cultural events, and Kildin Sami books have been printed in Norway, etc.

Fortunately, in the Murmansk region the minority groups are so small that there is little chance of ethnic conflicts breaking out, and stability will probably reign.

There are claims, however, that the aid given to the Sami is contributing to a separation of the Sami from the Komis (whose numbers are about the same as those of the Sami). I don't know how much truth there is in this, as I have never heard any complaints from a Komi. For decades, there has been a clear hierarchy among the minority groups in Lovozero. At the top are the Russians, then come the Komis, and at the bottom the Sami.

Contact with Scandinavian Sami has given considerable moral support to the Kola Sami. As a result, they have had the courage to stand up and demand the return of their rights which were taken away under Soviet rule. Today, the Russian authorities are undoubtedly more careful in their treatment of the Sami and other minority groups on Kola. Gone are the old slogans, such as "We are all one family. We all have equal rights".

The future of the Sami language on the Kola Peninsula is uncertain, but the Sami way of living will survive for a long time, even if the language is lost. The future for the Kola Sami looks brighter today than it did only a few years ago.

Leif Rantala,
Faculty of Education,
University og Capland,
Rovaniemi,
Finland.

Oil, gas and reindeer herding in the Nenets Autonomous Okrug

JOHNNY-LEO LUDVIKSEN

In April 1992, the then Norwegian foreign minister Thorvald Stoltenberg introduced the idea of a "Barents Region". The region was to provide a forum through which Norway, Sweden, Finland and Russia should be encouraged to increase cooperation and trade between their nations. Today, the Barents Region encompasses the counties of Nordland, Troms and Finnmark in Norway, Norrbotn in Sweden, Lappland Len in Finland, and Karel, Murmansk and Archangel Oblast in Russia.

The Barents Region can be termed a "region of natural resources". There are few regions in the world that can boast such huge reserves of oil, gas, minerals, hydroelectric power, fish and timber. In this article, we shall take a close look at the relationship between the oil industry and the reindeer industry in a region in NW Russia.

Oil and gas
National (Russian) and international oil companies have discovered huge reserves of oil and gas along the north coast of Russia, from Murmansk in the west to the Bering Strait in the east, a distance of nearly 7000 kilometres. The reserves are located primarily on the mainland, but significant gas fields have also been discovered in the Barents Sea, the Penchora Basin and the Kara Sea. Until now, most of the exploration has been concentrated on the mainland because extreme ice conditions complicate and increase the costs of any activity at sea.

Within the borders of the former Soviet Union are about 30.000 km of oil pipeline. They are of varying quality, and an estimated 9% of the oil in these pipelines leaks out every year. This is not only because they were badly built, but also because they have not been maintained since. In the west, it is usual to put aside 10% of the total running costs for future maintenance. In Russia the equivalent figure is 1–2%.

Exactly how much oil and gas is hidden under the Nenets Autonomous Okrug is uncertain. The figure increases each year and the latest estimates are 1.2 billion tonnes, including 2,500 billion cubic metres of gas in the Stokmanovskoje field in the Barents Sea. In the Rusanovskoje field in the Kara Sea, east of Novaya Zemlya, the gas reserves may be twice this amount (or four times those in the Norwegian Troll field in the North Sea). If we consider the whole of the Archangel Oblast, the available oil reserves may be as high as 1.2 billion tonnes, 489 billion cubic metres of gas and 20 billion tonnes of oil condensate.

The size of the reserves are so huge that it is not a question of if they will be expoilted, but when and at what scale.

Nenets Autonomous Okrug
The Nenets National Okrug was established in 1929, but the name was changed in 1977 to the Nenets Autonomous Okrug. This refres to a region which is more or less self–governed within the Oblast–regime. The Nenets Okrug covers an area of 176,700 square kilometres, which is equivalent to 54% of the area of Norway. Most of the okrug lies north of the Arctic Circle, in the northeast part of the Archangel Oblast.

Today, there is little oil activity in the region. In autumn 1994, the Nenets Okrug and the bordering parts of the Komi Republic were, however, hit by the first serious accident for many years. An old and badly maintained oil pipeline in Komi started to leak and released enormous quantities of crude oil across the tundra and into neighbouring rivers and streams. One of these rivers is the Pechora, which flows through the okrug and runs out into the Barents Sea. The size of the spill will first be determined after the spring thaw in 1995.

Nenets herding camp, August 1994. (Photo: Ivar Bjørklund).

The River Pechora runs south to north, dividing the Nenets Okrug into two. In the eastern part, detailed geological surveys have been carried out for a couple of decades, and large reserves of oil have been found. This will have important economic consequences for such a poor region where unemployment levels are high, the standard of living is well under the average for Russia and infrastructure is lacking.

Less than fifty thousand people live in the Nenets Autonomous Okrug. Of these, 6,500 are Nenets. The tundra is the home of the Nenets, one of 26 native tribes in northern Russia. Most of the Nenets live in small villages (posjolok – each of 70–1200 inhabitants) out on the tundra . Of a total of 30 villages, only one is inhabited by Nenets only (Varnek on the island Vaigatsj). The others include a mixture of Nenets, Koma and Russians.

Reindeer herding and collectives
Each village is organized as a collective, and most of them base their existence on reindeer herding, with hunting and fishing as important secondary sources of living. After the collectivization in the middle of the 1930s, the organization of the reindeer herding changed from the traditional system of several private flocks to a single, large flock owned by the collective and herded by work gangs. Reindeer herding became an important part of the sector–organized planned economy. The philosophy was that the herders out on the tundra would also participate in the development of the Soviet states. A normal collective in this region is made up of 7–8 work gangs who herd 15–18,000 reindeer, of which about 4,500 are slaughtered each year. In comparison to the Scandinavian system, this is a high level of meat production. The local administration claim, however, that the collectives are not profitable enough, and that more money could be earned through oil and gas production.

The low profitability of reindeer herding is, however, closely associated with the development of the Russian economy in general. As is known, the Russians are in great difficulties at present, and the rate of inflation is sky high. At the same time, Russia has joined the international oil market, which has resulted in a marked increase in the price of fuel oils. This directly affects the costs of freight, especially air freight which, in turn, has resulted in a large reduction in the use of helicopters and planes. The consequences of this are easy to imagine in a region where there are no roads and where all transport of people is by air.

High inflation rates have also caused problems for the reindeer owners who have chosen to withdraw from the collectives and set up independently. Like everyone else, they have problems in finding transport in to Naryan Mar, the main meat market of the region. In addition, they face two bigger problems. The first is that Naryan Mar is not obliged to buy their meat, and if the combine does so, the prices are open to negotiation. The herders have thus a choice of selling their meet to the combine at below market prices, or selling the meat privately. There are, however, few customers out on the tundra, and they generally choose to sell at deflated prices. The second problem arises through the annual cycle of reindeer herding in that all slaughtering takes place in November. This results in one large pay packet a year. With today's inflation rate, this means that the pay they receive in November is nearly worthless 3–4 months later. Any money that they have failed to exchange for a more stable currency is thus lost. As a result, there are several herders with two years experience of the "capitalist system" who now wish to rejoin the collective.

Oil and gas
Within the oil industry the situation is quite the reverse. Here optimism is high, and the local authorities are more than aware that oil means money in nearly empty state coffers. A simple start in the most promising fields in the region could result in an increase in income from 5 million to 150 million dollars a year! In addition, many new jobs will be created, modern technology will be brought to the region and an explosive development of the infrastructure can be expected. The county already has contact with several international oil companies which are training Russian personnel and bringing in new technical equipment. This contact is also important as a sign to the central administration in Archangel that the okrug wishes to retain its autonomy. The relationship between the Archangel Oblast and the Nenets Okrug is, as yet, not fully clarified. But one thing is certain: the important decisions concerning the exploitation of oil in the okrug are made in Naryan Mar and not in Archangel.

Drilling sites on the tundra.
(Photo: Johnny-Leo Ludviksen).

The future
With these enormous sources of income in mind, one important question comes to mind. Are "hard currency" and increased incomes the best solution to the problems faced by the local inhabitants? What will they live on when the oil runs out? Shouldn't such regions have several sources of income, not just oil?

Furthermore, has the reindeer industry any possibility of surviving and developing side by side with the oil industry? It is difficult to give a straight answer to these questions, but four important factors should at least be taken into consideration.

First, the seismological surveys which are already in progress on the tundra are causing a lot of ecological damage. In the Nenets Autonomous Okrug, as elsewhere in Russia, these surveys are made using caterpillar tractors. This form of transport causes irreparable damage to the surface of the tundra through a process called thermocast. This process involves the removal of the surface layers of moss which insulate the underlying permofrost, and the subsequent melting of the permafrost during the warm summer months. The end result is a bog–like area which is useless as grazing grounds for at least 100 years. Such areas are already evident where the traffic is heaviest, e.g. near the various oil bases.

An abandoned drilling site showing the local destruction of the ecosystem. (Photo: Johnny-Leo Ludviksen).

Second, the actual oil or gas production will cause even greater problems. Any oil that is produced must be transported out of the region to the national or world market. The problem is, how? One possibility is to build expensive pipelines southwards to the existing oil fields in the Komi Republic. Another, which the oil companies are considering, is to build oil terminals on the north coast of Pechora Bay. Three sites are being looked at, but all of them will neccessitate an extensive construction of pipelines. Any pipelines built on an east–west axis will have serious consequences for reindeer herding throughout the entire district in that they will block the reindeers' trek routes between their summer and winter pastures. To persuade flocks of thousands of reindeer to cross 5– 10 pipelines will be extremely difficult.

Thirdly, any development of the oilfields will probably affect the settlement pattern in the region. Already today areas of damaged tundra, abandoned oil rigs and other industrial waste which are spread over large areas have forced the reindeer herders to seek other trek routes or even cease to use the area at all. Since most of the reindeer herding is organized in collectives, with a line of provisioning out to the work gangs from the central village, the destruction of grazing land could result in whole villages being abandoned. There are today no alternative grazing areas, and the question arises as to whether the reindeer industry can survive in its present form.

The tundra is the backbone of the Nenets way of life. (Photo: Ivar Bjørklund).

And finally, the argument in favour of developing these regions is economic. As mentioned earlier, the Nenets' economy is failing but, along with the poorly developed infrastructure, it could be saved by oil money. Experience from other regions of the world show, however, that an increase in income is not always the way to create jobs for the people of the north.

This was clearly shown in Alaska. There, steering committees were nominated with representatives from all the settlements affected by oil development. These settlements each received part of the oil income and, as a result, developed rapidly with the building of new schools, arts centres, swimming pools, etc. The inhabitants who earlier earned their living by hunting and fishing became oilmen. This resulted in employment for everyone in the early phases, and levels of income rose considerably. But when the development stage came to an end and the oil profits started to drop, the numbers of jobs also started to diminish. As a rule, the locals were the first to lose their jobs as they were generally the least skilled. This soon resulted in huge economic problems for individual families and the local communities as a whole. The latter were landed with a mass of new buildings and maintenance costs which thy could no longer afford.

Afanasi Semjonovitsj Valej, Darja Alexandrovna Laptander and daughter Oksana. (Photo: Ivar Bjørklund).

What perhaps surprized people most was that the billions of oil dollars failed to provide a single permanent job locally. In other words, the authorities in the Nenets Okrug face huge challenges. Will they be able to manage the oil and gas reserves in such a way that they simultaneously and in the long run maintain the locals' economic and cultural interests ? Or will the oil development become a "klondyke" in which the rules and regulations are laid down by the foreign oil companies and short–term profit motives? As yet it is too early to guess. But not a single analysis has been made of the consequences that any oil development may have on the region's most important source of income at present, namely the reindeer industry.

**Johnny-Leo Ludviksen,
Institute of Social Science,
University of Tromsø,
9037 Tromsø.**

A Journey to the Bolshezemelskaja Tundra

IVAR BJØRKLUND

Towards the end of February 1994, I left the mining town of Vorkuta in a snowmobile heading for "The Big Tundra" – Bolshezemelskaja Tundra – the huge barren land between the Pechora River and the Ural Mountains. In former times this area was called Western Siberia, a reference to its climatic and ethnographic similarities with the area east of the Urals. As far back as we know, this tundra has been the homeland of the Nenets – one of the largest indigenous groups in the Russian north. But it has also been one of the main strongholds of reindeer herding – an important economic adaptation in the northern hemisphere.

As we headed northwards, it became clear why the tundra had become the last resort of the Nenets. Earlier they used to live in the forest area to the south. But aggression from the Komi people and a growing Russian expansion forced them to withdraw north of the tree line during the last centuries. With the exception of a small group of Nenets living in the forest along the river Ob, the Nenets of today live on the tundra – from the Kanin peninsula in the west to the eastern banks of the Jenisei River. The Big Tundra west of the Urals has so far been an area suitable only for reindeer herding and some hunting and fishing. The Komi settlers along the large rivers to the south never cared much for these barren areas and the Komi reindeer herding groups only used it for summer pastures. In the winter they moved down the lichen-rich areas below the tree line.

In Russian folklore, the tundra is regarded as the ultimate wilderness, a world of its own beyond civilization. A perfect setting for *gulags*, social outcasts – and indigenous groups. Being the masters of reindeer herding – an adaptation in which the Russians have never involved themselves – groups like the Nenets became the sole inhabitants of the enormous tundra. Until now, their pastoral knowledge and technology was the only way to utilise the resources of the area. But in the last couple of decades, new resources such as oil and gas have been discovered on the tundra and their exploitation is now high on the economic agenda of the Russian authorities. The known oil and gas reserves of Yamal and Bolshezemelskaja Tundra – the heartland of the Nenets – are considered to be some of the biggest in the world, and international oil companies have been wooing Russian authorities for a quite some time.

71

None of this was regarded as bad news by Ilya, the Nenets reindeer herder who accompanied us in the snowmobile heading for his camp way out on the tundra. He had invited us to come along to see his family and "how we live", after I had met him last summer during a field trip near the coast of the Kara Sea. Ilya was a man with a strong interest in the ways of modern life, especially when it came to technology. He was on good terms with the oil men working for the oil companies and gave and received many a favour throughout the year. Living in the Bolshezemelskaja Tundra all the year round meant that transportation was a never–ending problem. Here the helicopters and the land vehicles of the oil companies represented a handy way to get a ride to a neighbour or the nearest village. And as for the drilling towers, many a herder regarded them as important landmarks which made navigation quite easier when travelling in this incredibly flat landscape.

That the oil-companies – or Russian authorities, for that sake – knew nothing about the Nenetsy way of life was regarded as a matter of course. But Ilya and his group did not know much about Russian society either, and that was becoming more and more of a problem now that the whole country was in a state of flux. This particular group of Nenets – two hundred persons – had a long and rather dramatic relationship with Russian authorities. During the years of collectivization, they ran away with their herds and actually fought the Russians with arms. They managed to stay away from the collective farms and stuck to

---

Ilya and his driving team.
(Photo: Ivar Bjørklund).

their own way of living out on the tundra. The authorities never caught up with them, and as the years passed by, they became "non-existent". They isolated themselves from Russian society, their children never went to school and the men never did their military service. Because they were never registered – neither births nor deaths – they were able to continue their lives as they had done long before the revolution. They lived on the tundra all year around, only visiting a village maybe once or twice a year to buy necessary provisions like tea, flour, butter etc. This lifestyle was necessary as long as the Soviet regime existed. Because their reindeer herding was family based, they were by definition practising private ownership – something which did not exist under the Russian constitution. So if anybody in the regional administration knew about their existence, they were not keen to mention the fact that a group of "capitalistic" reindeer herders had been roaming the tundra ever since the revolution. But now the Soviet state has gone and capitalism is on everybody's agenda. As a result, Ilya and his group could present themselves as the new models when it came to reindeer herding.

If it was Ilya's interest in the world around him which made him decide to invite a Norwegian anthropologist along, then it probably was his interest in the world beyond which also led him to bring two Jehova's Witness missionaries. He had met them in Vorkuta and immediately invited them to his camp. They gave him a Russian Bible and as the only literate person in the camp, Ilya spent quite some time discussing this new gospel. The religious beliefs of the Nenets were not that simple for everybody to grasp. In the ethnographical literature it is referred to as shamanism; in their daily life they referred to it as a complex cosmology where the power of nature played an important part. It became pretty clear that our missionary companions regarded the natives as straight–forward pagans, and their mission was to save their souls.

So here we were; an anthropologist and two missionaries on our way to visit one of the last groups of natives who more or less had managed to remain outside Russian society. It was, of course, not the first time anthropology and Christianity came to ride the same bandwagon, literally speaking. But I always thought it a phenomenon of a colonial past, a reference to politics and ideologies no one wishes to be associated with anymore. The only one who seemed happy with the situation was Ilya. The closer we came to the camp, the more he engaged in planning the details of the festivities ahead of us. We would slaughter two reindeer, he said, one in the way it was done in Norway and one in the Nenets way. Then we would prepare dishes in our respective traditions and have a big meal.

It was a nice idea, and when we arrived at the camp in the evening, we immediately put his plan into practice. The camp consisted of two tents, Ilya and his parents in one and his sister, brother-in-law and their children in the other. The tents were made of two layers of

73

reindeer skin with a stove in the middle. Outside it was –35⁰C with a bitterly cold wind, inside it was rather warm – as long as there was enough firewood. Because there was no wood to be found on the tundra, long expeditions had to be taken to the Kara Sea coast for driftwood.

The reindeer herd was divided into two parts, one of which grazed peacefully around the camp. We lassooed a yearling, slaughtered it in a way which the Nenets thought rather cruel and messy and started to prepare the dishes we were used to from Norway. We decided upon blood sausages, by our tastes a delicious treat. In the meantime the missionaries were busy unpacking glossy booklets telling about the wonders of Jehova, illustrated with pictures of suburban life in sunny California.

We found the camp way out on the barren tundra. (Photo: Ivar Bjørklund).

While the intestines were washed, I started to whip the blood which I had collected from the animal. Because of the cold, these preparations had to be done inside, and the tent was soon crammed with curious people watching our enterprise with great interest. But suddenly a demanding voice from one of the missionaries told me to stop my undertaking and consider the sins I was about to bring upon these innocent people. I immediately asked what was going on and was given a citation from the Old Testament regarding a ban from God on the consumption of blood. To eat the food I was preparing was the uttermost sin. Now we had a problem. The missionaries and their idea of damnation was something I could live with. But their persistence put our hosts in an akward position. They had asked some of the guests to present themselves through the food they made. Now the other group of guests made this gesture into a question of life and death. The Nenets immediately sensed the growing conflict. They did not say a word, only listened to the more and more intense discussion between their guests. Ilya, who spoke fluent Russian, might have given a thought to the Nenets' practice of drinking blood, but he said nothing. The missionaries, on the other hand, made it clear that eating blood was the uttermost denial of God's laws – explicitly forbidden in the Bible they were citing from. Ilya, however, was a man with well developed diplomatic skills. He threw some salt and flour into the kettle, declared that it thereby no longer could be considered as pure blood and thus not a violation of the Holy Book they so kindly had given him.

Thus the row came to an end. The women in the tent prepared the table, which soon became quite a buffet filled as it was with different kinds of meat, fish, berries, bread – and blood sausages. While the missionaries presented colour pictures of nuclear families in front of their bungalows in Los Angeles, Ilya's father launched into an epic song about the mammoths. It turned out to be their myth of creation, a long and fascinating story about burning rivers and people fighting mammoths. Our host's father was about 65 years old and the oldest Nenet around. He had lived through

Semjon Ivanovitsj Taibarei, Alexandra Semjonova Valei and two of their children. (Photo: Ivar Bjørklund).

almost the whole Soviet era and had some vivid stories to tell. The collectivization policy met strong resistance in the Russian north. It was not until the end of the Second World War that the authorities caught up with this group of Nenets :

"We were camping near the river Khare-jakha when the rumours came that private owners would be deprived of their herds. As soon as we heard the news we collected the herd and moved. We had nothing to stay for. We crossed the river Sibert-ju by boats and came to Obskaya Guba (on the other side the river Ob). We camped at Aksarka, where we thought they could not catch us. But they had sent a telegram from Amderma (an army base in the north) to Aksarka, and we were stopped. They made us cut wood and transport it on our sledges to the village. They promised us bread. I remember it was very cold. When we were cold, we warmed ourselves in the snow.

Our clothes were worn out, our *malitsas* (furcoats) were without fur, and our *pimis* (footwear) were torn. We were in rags, but nobody laughed at us. The Nenets (in the village) understood that we had no other clothes and the Russians thought that everything was as it should be. I had no shirt under my malitsa. And there our reindeer began to die. So we decided that we would put an end to all this. As soon as the ice on the river had broken up, we left the place and went

---

All parents were rather worried for the prospects for their children in the age of oil industry. (Photo: Ivar Bjørklund).

north. We crossed the Ural Mountains and reached the Kara Sea. All our food was gone when we came to the river Khalmer-ju. We went to the village of Ust-Kara and there we bartered meat and skins for tobacco, matches and food."

At this time many groups of Nenets in the Bolshezemelskaja Tundra had the same type of experiences with the Russian authorities. The enforced collectivization met strong resistance and many groups tried to hide themselves from the authorities. Because "The Great Patriotic War" was then being fought, Russian authority was probably slack in the area and the Nenets seized the opportunity. They united, armed themselves with whatever was at hand and started to fight the Russians. This revolt was called the Mandela, and many Nenets today talk about it as their own revolution against the Soviet power. The actual events are rather hard to describe today, as all the Nenets participants were either killed or disappeared in prison camps. It has also been pointed out that the revolt might have been provoked by internal struggles for power within the local Russian authority. But according to Ilya and his family, it was a full–scale warfare:

"Whole families had to join the Mandela. If somebody refused, he was prosecuted and killed. The Mandela members guarded their territory and built a fortress of stones in the Urals. Children were sent to watch the herds and the grown-up men discussed strategy in the tents. They had a shaman; he played the drum and tried to foresee the future. The Russians started to take pictures of the Mandela people from planes. One of these small planes flew from Amderma. They had a Nenets man aboard, he knew all the reindeerherders in the tundra. They took pictures of the people and he told the names of those in the picture. They took pictures of the fortress too. They organized people in Amderma, armed them and prepared to fight the Mandela. They were told that a new war had begun. They attacked the fortress with machine guns and finally they captured everyone. On the battlefield you can still see two skulls – they shine as though they have been polished.

Water was made from melting ice. (Photo: Ivar Bjørklund).

All except the small children were arrested. Later they arrested innocent people who had not been in the Mandela. The Mandela began in spring and by August everyone was under arrest. There are no people left on the tundra today who took part in the Mandela, only the shaman's son. But he does not want to talk about the Mandela, because he is afraid of being arrested himself."

It was a dramatic story, one of the many which illustrate the epic struggle for survival among the Nenets. Whether they were fighting mammoths or Russian authorities, their stories – which were often presented through songs – would explain in detail how they survived. They could go on singing them for hours – they all knew them by heart and it was a valued way to spend leisure time. I told them about Norway, a country they knew just as little about as Norwegians knew about the Nenets. But Ilya told me he once had a shotgun, which his grandfather purchased from a Norwegian merchant who came to Novaja Zemlia "more than a hundred years ago". His grandfather was one of the group of Nenets which the Tsar sent to Novaja Zemlja in the 1870s, to establish a permanent population on the island. Norwegian trappers had been living there for quite some time and the Russians were afraid that Norway might claim the whole island. The Nenets found the conditions favourable and made a good living out of hunting, trapping and reinder herding.

A buffet was made for all guests. (Photo: Ivar Bjørklund).

Ilya's grandfather used to tell about the first ship which came to the island from the west. When the captain discovered all the fur among the Nenets, he wanted to trade – but he had no goods to offer. The Nenets, however, liked the man and told him that he could pay them back next year. In August the ship returned westwards. Next year the ship came back – together with two other ships. And they were all loaded with all kinds of goods: rifles, ammunition, ropes, butter, knives, etc. Now it was the Nenets' turn to be in debt. They did not have enough fur to pay for all these valuables, and an agreement was made that the ships should return the next year and be paid then. All the modern equipment increased the efficiency of their hunting and trapping and a lot of fur was waiting for the Norwegians when the spring came. But the captain did not return and nobody has seen either him or anybody else from the west ever since.

Today the most important problem on the tundra is the question of land. Privatization and the collapse of state control have put land up for grabs. The collective farms have long been negotiating with the regional authorities to have their pastures regulated and secured. Borders are drawn up and papers issued. At the same time, oil companies are presenting their claims regarding drilling sites and pipelines. Norwegians are again doing business with the Nenets. But this time it is not fur they are trading – sea captains are replaced by Norsk Hydro and Saga Petroleum. Together with other foreign oil-companies, they have invested millions of dollars in the area. The American company Conoco alone is planning to invest 3 billion dollars in the region. The potential is enormous. The oil-production potential in Nenets A. Okrug is forecast to be of the same size as the potential in Norway. Since almost half of the foreign currency income in Russia comes from the export of oil, there will be few objections from the Russian authorities to realize the potential.

Faced with this situation, Ilya and his group are put in an akward position. Being "non-existent" according to the Russian bureaucracy, they have no

All are dressed in fur from top to toe. (Photo: Ivar Bjørklund).

rights. They can not even prove their own existence, because they are not registered anywhere. And not being registered and thus not even having an I.D. card, they are – to put it mildly – in an impossible situation in Russian society. If in addition you are illiterate and isolated from any means of communication, your possibilities become rather minute – especially if you are facing international oil companies operating within a collapsing state. So far nobody has made any analyses of the Nenets' legal and economic situation. None of the oil companies have looked into what consequences the oil activity might have on the herding operations, and no authority has made any references to international law protecting indigenous groups and human rights.

Ivar Bjørklund,
Tromsø Museum,
University of Tromsø,
9037 Tromsø.